BUILDING BLOCKS OF BEHAVIOUR IN EARLY CHILDHOOD

BUILDING BLOCKS OF BEHAVIOUR IN EARLY CHILDHOOD

KERRY MURPHY
SARAH DOYLE

Sage

Sage

3rd Floor
HYLO
103–105 Bunhill Row
London, EC1Y 8LZ

2455 Teller Road
Thousand Oaks
California 91320

10th Floor, Emaar Capital Tower
2 MG Road, Sikanderpur, Sector 26
Gurugram, Haryana – 122002
India

8 Marina View Suite 43-053
Asia Square Tower 1
Singapore 018960

Editor: Amy Thornton
Senior project editor: Chris Marke
Cover design: Wendy Scott
Typeset by: C&M Digitals (P) Ltd, Chennai, India
Printed in the UK

British Library Cataloguing in Publication Data

A catalogue record for this book is available from the British Library

ISBN 978-1-5297-7831-1
ISBN 978-1-5297-7830-4 (pbk)

Contents

About the authors

Kerry Murphy is an early childhood specialist with a background in neurodiversity, disability and behaviour. She is an Associate Lecturer at Goldsmiths University, London, and freelance trainer. She is currently completing her doctorate (EdD) exploring how neurodiversity-informed pedagogies can mobilise early educators to disrupt ableism. Kerry's aim in working in the Early Years is to challenge the deficit narratives about children whose development does not take a typical pathway. She adopts a neurodiversity-affirming stance and believes in strengths-led approaches to inclusion. She offers training and guidance via a project called Diverse Pathways for Early Childhood which is a collective creating neurodiversity-affirming tools and resources for Early Years, schools and specialist settings. She is the author of several books on neurodiversity in early childhood.

Sarah Doyle is an experienced special educational needs (SEN) consultant and an Early Years adviser. She has experience as a local authority Early Years Consultant, with responsibility for leading the development of high-quality inclusive provision in a range of education settings. Sarah plans and delivers Early Years professional training including behaviour in the Early Years, supporting play and learning and developing effective SEN provision. As a freelance SEN consultant, Sarah has worked with a range of organisations, providing direct support and guidance to Early Years and specialist settings, children, young people and families. Her personal experience as a proud parent of a neurodivergent son informs her approach. Sarah's work in the Early Years also includes advising on inclusive practice, the role of the SENCO, SEND strategy and policy.

About this book

We wrote this book to share insights into how we have come to understand and support children's behaviour. When writing, we wanted to address the nuance and reality of trying to co-regulate with multiple children. We both know what it is like to work in the Early Years and the emotional, physical, social and mental labour it requires, so we wanted to create a resource that acts as a supportive companion and a guidebook for those tricky moments.

We would like to thank . . . all the 'naughty' children who have taught us so much!

There is so much more to say about behaviour in the Early Years than can be covered in the pages of any book. As educators, we are always learning from the children in our care and this is always changing. This book shares our unique perspective and aims to provide a springboard for you to explore other thinkers and advocates to deepen your own pedagogy.

For more advice, support and professional learning, go to **www.diversepathways.org** where we offer a range of free resources and tools for supporting behaviour. You can also follow us on instagram: **@diversepathways_earlyyears**

Introduction

Why behaviour?

One of the main reasons we decided to write this book is that, throughout our years of working in early childhood education, concerns about children's behaviour and how to support actively and sensitively repeatedly come up, often invoking quite emotional responses in early educators and teachers. Caring for and educating children is incredibly joyful and meaningful, but it can also be complex and contradictory. Having both been early educators on the ground for many years, we have acutely felt the emotional, social, physical and mental labour of caregiving and education. When we moved into consultancy roles, we were aware that we did not want to lose sight that this is incredibly difficult work at times, and we have never wanted to present an idealised view of behaviour support. We also have often felt that the early educators' emotional experiences can get lost in the discussion.

Children's observable and externalised behaviours, which are influenced by many factors such as their energy, sensory systems, sensations, thoughts, feeling and emotions and lived experiences can make educators feel confused, de-skilled, frustrated and triggered. Educators often feel judged for having these feelings, but it is important to understand that human relationships and attachments are a dynamic (and messy) process. While plentiful positive experiences are essential for building strong social and emotional foundations, this does not mean the absence of stressful or adverse experiences (unfortunately). This applies to us as educators as much as it does to the children in our care.

As educators, we may not be able to shield children from every challenge or stressful situation they encounter, but we do play an important role in sensitively preparing them to navigate these moments while maintaining their good mental health. To do this, we must also have the capacity to maintain and manage our own mental health, wellbeing and welldoing. This is an active and ongoing process which takes practice. Many factors can influence our capacity to maintain good mental health when supporting young children, and this book attempts to unpick the experience of both children and educators to establish deeper connections in supporting behaviour. We recently saw a quote that said, 'regulation isn't taught, it is co-created' (author unknown) and while we both agreed, we also felt that it is safe to say it is both – though, we feel that the latter often gets somewhat overlooked in education. For example, there is a tendency for us to pass on and teach our skills of self-regulation so the child can do everything independently. But humans exist in networks and co-create communities and spaces where regulation climates are varied and always connected in some way.

(Mis)behaviour is inevitable in all of us ...

In our numerous conversations, we realised that to write a book about behaviour, we also had to be transparent about how behaviour in young children has made us feel and how we have perhaps previously reacted, when we wanted to sensitively respond. We have been careful not to present an idealised view on how to support behaviour or to suggest that there is a universal set of strategies that will work to resolve all behaviours that we might define as undesirable or unacceptable. The truth is, there are countless reasons and functions behind our human behaviours. But we have a tendency as adults to separate our own (mis)behaviours from children's as though we have outgrown the capacity to throw a wobble, talk back, act out or be impulsive. Yes, we might have more maturity and skills to manage those behaviours, but all humans have the capacity to draw on (mis)behaviours to make sense of themselves and the world around them. Our goal is to understand what might be happening in relation to those behaviours and to think about that network of regulation and how it can scaffold our emotional wellbeing so that we can then do well too. By being there with children during their trickiest moments, we help make sense of their actions and guide them towards autonomy and ultimately a deeper understanding of themselves.

Some confessions ...

To set the tone for this book, it is useful to begin with some confessions to emphasise that we are not writing this book as wise owls or fountains of knowledge who have it all figured out. We still struggle with behaviour too. Our confessions:

1 We both find children's behaviours annoying, frustrating and triggering at times. We have acknowledged that sometimes behaviours can make us feel panicked and de-skilled.
2 We have not always supported behaviours well; we still make mistakes and still forget our own advice and learning.
3 Sometimes, children's behaviours stir up uncomfortable feelings for us both. We have disliked, resented and blamed children for their behaviours, especially when feeling stressed. We have then felt guilt and shame over it.
4 Sometimes when we are asked for advice about children's behaviour, we have no idea about the 'answer' because we are also still learning, and we are reluctant to advise on children who we don't know and have never met.
5 We want every child to feel seen, heard and understood with unconditional positive high regard. We also want educators to feel seen, heard and understood with unconditional positive high regard.

You might wonder why you would pick up a book by two people who openly admit to facing these struggles. It is precisely because we are honest about these challenges that we invite you to keep reading. In our own training, we noticed a tendency for educators to stay silent about the discomfort and frustration that can come with high-intensity behaviours. They often choose to stay positive or pretend they like every child no matter what. But for us, that is simply not the reality. We want educators to dig deeper and truly reflect on the complexity of relationships and attachments with children in early childhood settings. In fact, research tells us that when those in caregiving roles engage with their complex emotions the risks of exhaustion and burnout are reduced and they become better at the caregiving role (Pisaniello et al., 2012).

Venting versus processing

It is important to clarify that we are in no way suggesting that educators should vent, speak or act inappropriately about or towards children or their behaviours. That approach is unhelpful and can lead to unfair labels and negative perceptions of young children. Instead, to understand behaviour, we should not ignore our own feelings about it. Rather, we should find healthy ways to process and make sense of those emotions. By doing this, we model the very skills we aim to teach children: how to understand and manage their feelings in constructive and pro-social ways.

The way to develop these constructive habits is to develop an understanding about why young children use behaviour as a means of letting us know that something is happening for them. Behaviours are a handy tool to let someone know relatively quickly that there is a need, a disgruntle or emotion surfacing. Using the analogy of building blocks, each chapter will build upon your understanding and include key features so that you can navigate your way to effective behaviour support that is rooted in understanding a child's emotional, social, physical and sensory experiences.

Chapter features

Throughout the book, we have used the following pedagogical features:

Provocations: A starting point to get you thinking

Each chapter begins with a provocation to introduce you to an idea, concept or reflection. This serves as a springboard for your thinking and helps to frame the intent and focus of the chapter.

Behaviour blueprint: Going from old to new ways of thinking

This feature makes visible the dominant narratives and traditional assumptions that have shaped behaviour practice, before offering a reframed, attuned way of understanding behaviour. It supports a shift away from compliance-led models towards relational, developmental and neurodiversity-affirming perspectives.

Put it into practice: Tips and techniques that you can try out

These short, practical ideas support you to translate theory into everyday practice. Each practical tip is designed to be realistic, immediately usable and possible for you to try the very next day with real children in real environments.

Case studies: Hearing practical examples and reflections

Case studies bring concepts to life through real-world scenarios drawn from Early Years practice. Each one illustrates how behaviour, context and developmental pathways interact, while modelling an attuned response.

Activities: Reflective activities to help you build stronger understandings

These activities show how adults can actively scaffold behaviour through environment, interaction and relational support. They offer structured opportunities for individual or team-based exploration and help you translate principles into sustained practice.

Intersectionality insights: Exploring bias and marginalisation

These insights draw attention to how behaviour is interpreted differently depending on race, gender, disability and other intersecting identities. They highlight how bias can shape adult responses and children's experiences, especially for marginalised groups. By surfacing these dynamics, the book encourages equity-driven, anti-bias behavioural support.

Signposts and references: Deepen your learning

These provide you with key academic, practical and lived-experience sources to extend your understanding. The signposts direct you towards further reading that aligns with the book's ethos of attunement, anti-ableism and developmental grounding, ensuring the work sits within a rigorous, credible and diverse knowledge base.

A note on language

In this book we have made a few language choices that we hope are in-tune and sensitive to children's unique experiences. There has been debate on whether the focus on external behaviours ends up overshadowing the underlying emotional experiences and needs of the child. In our view, we need to write about both because what has been externalised can be a gateway or insight into what might be happening underneath the surface. We also find that looking beyond behaviours is unrealistic when they are usually the thing that has the greatest impact on the collective experiences of a group.

This book will also explore the behaviours and developmental experiences of children who are neurodivergent and disabled. Throughout the book, we combine identity-first language (autistic child) with person-first language (child with Down syndrome) to try to reflect community preferences. We also acknowledge that language preferences are unique and we attempt to offer a balanced approach in the way we use language.

Is this book for me?

Kerry: Recently I delivered a lecture to students on a PGCE programme on the issues with behaviour management in schools. As I was delivering the lecture, I noticed that one student looked visibly angry over the content. At the end of the lecture, he sat with me and explained that he didn't know why exactly, but he felt very triggered by my beliefs on children's behaviour. He felt that I was trying to influence him by openly criticising those who believe that behaviour needs to be controlled. We had a very in-depth discussion where we could acknowledge that we held different views about behaviour, and he came back to me a week later to let me know he read up on some key researchers and advocates of behaviourist approaches and they aligned more with his beliefs. Our ideas diverged and we had to acknowledge that this is a reality of the education system. We do need to make space for a network of perspectives, positionalities and pedagogies with the hope of developing practices that are flexible and reflective of the diversity of the world we live in. Our main motivation is that our decisions are driven by the best interests of the child.

Positionality

Sarah and I take a particular positionality across this book that may or may not align with your current perspective. This book is not just to inform, but to help you interrogate how you lead with children's best interests. However, we are aware that sometimes our positionalities can diverge to such a degree that it may be worth exploring the below reflection statements to think about where you currently stand. For each statement, ask yourself if you agree or disagree.

- I believe that we should use punitive/rule-based systems to control behaviour.
- I believe that behaviours are mostly intentional and should be stopped.
- I believe children should be held fully responsible for their actions and should accept the consequences.
- I do not believe that behaviours occur because children have unmet needs.

- I believe that boundaries keep children safe in order to explore their emotional experiences.
- I believe that behaviour needs to be shaped, reinforced and fixed.
- I believe that there are acceptable and unacceptable behaviours.
- I believe rules should be enforced without exception.
- I believe that children should be excluded for their undesirable behaviours.
- I believe that behaviour is something all humans are always learning to manage.
- I believe the best way to manage behaviour is to have rewards, sanctions and rules.

If you predominately disagreed with these statements, this book probably already aligns with your positionality. If you largely agreed, then this book may offer challenge and provocation, or a different perspective. Either way, we encourage you to keep reading.

References

Pisaniello, S.L., Winefield, H.R. and Delfabbro, P.H. (2012) The influence of emotional labour and emotional work on the occupational health and wellbeing of South Australian hospital nurses. *Journal of Vocational Behavior*, 80(3), 579–91.

Before we begin

The building blocks of behaviour attunement

To guide you through this book, we wanted to share with you our *principles of behaviour attunement*. Behaviour attunement refers to the recognition that a child's actions, reactions and responses often serve as the most obvious signal that there is a need or stressor. By acknowledging the behaviour while tuning into what might be happening at a deeper level for the child, we are then able to identify approaches, techniques and responses that are more compatible. For us, this is the alternative to behaviour management, offering us a more effective and sustainable approach, which helps us to connect more deeply with children during their trickiest moments. You may use and return to these principles as a guide as you make your way through the book.

- We all (mis)behave.
- Behaviour is learning in action.
- Self-regulation is a lifelong process, not a development outcome.
- You can't regulate sensations and emotions if you are not allowed to experience them.
- Behaviour gives us information and clues.
- Behaviour can be self-advocacy and rightful resistance.
- Behaviours don't have to make sense to us right away.
- We *all* deserve access to regulation, rest and repair.

Block one: *We all (mis)behave ...*

We often speak with Early Years educators about the behavioural expectations placed on children. Many refer to the ways developmental norms can lead to the idea that for a child to be considered well-behaved, they must consistently show compliance. And yet, when we ask if they could meet the developmental norms of children, they often say 'no' or 'with difficulty'. For example, we still have an education system that suggests stillness and sedentary behaviour are key indicators for paying attention. But most children and adults would find whole-body listening (sitting still, quiet hands, quiet feet, locked mouths, eyes looking) very challenging to consistently achieve. Furthermore, we know that movement often supports attention and engagement. As Sally Neaum reminds us 'children do not learn to sit still by sitting still' (Neaum, 2021, p. 9).

Similarly, if you asked most adults who were feeling the emotion of anger to remain calm while being angry, they may find it very challenging because they may need to express their anger in a charged way. The opposite of calm isn't necessarily chaos; it's alertness. Many expectations we impose on children can be unrealistic and too developmentally normative, especially when we apply expectations in a blanket manner. We also often forget that misbehaviour is an inevitable and healthy part of being human and serves as a good way to make sense of things. The difference between adults and children is that we often have plenty more allowable misbehaviours in adulthood because we are not under the same surveillance as children. We want to highlight two everyday examples of adult misbehaviour, and how easily we accept and accommodate this in ourselves and others as part of the human experience.

Anyone who has ventured on the London Underground will know that grown adults misbehave *all the time*. Whether it be pushing past each other, tutting under our breaths at someone getting a seat before us, or shouting at tourists to get out of the way. This misbehaviour in most cases is not necessarily a sign that as adults we are all naughty and anti-social. Rather, there are contexts and situations where, even as adults, we can struggle to manage ourselves. We likely attribute our disgruntled behaviours to a long day at work, or tiredness, or overstimulation. In short, we don't judge ourselves or others too harshly. We don't put ourselves in time-out.

Let's take another example. I, Kerry, have a reputation for being badly behaved in meetings. I find them boring and I will fidget, play on my phone, take multiple toilet breaks or try to find some light relief. When Sarah and I worked together, I would often try to distract her in meetings for some comedic relief. Why? Because I could not sit and focus for the number of hours the meeting required. As adults, we might not necessarily feel comfortable to say, 'I find these meetings boring and so I need to find ways to regulate to satisfy the boredom.' So, in this scenario, as adults we often comply more than children, as a child is likely to let us know if they are bored, or distracted. The social rules have not yet been enforced on the child.

So why have we chosen these two contrasting examples? We wanted to highlight that we are not that different from the children we care for and educate. As humans, misbehaviour serves a function and while we need to maintain and moderate our behaviours, we also need to accept them as part of human experience. Rather than an education that focuses on suppressing children's behaviours, we need one that helps children to make sense of the complexities of human behaviour.

Block two: *Behaviour is learning in action ...*

Consider the following (from Rypple, 2021):

- if a child can't yet write ... *we teach*
- if a child can't yet read ... *we teach*

- if a child can't yet tie up their shoelaces ... *we teach*
- if a child can't yet climb ... *we teach*

but

- if a child cannot yet 'behave' ... *we* ...

One of the most transformational shifts in our practice came when we began to fully embrace behaviour as *learning in action*. This doesn't mean that behaviours aren't sometimes confronting or challenging (and annoying), but viewing them through this lens invites curiosity rather than a drive for compliance. Think about it this way: if we treated learning behaviours like learning to write your name, the contrast becomes clear. When a child struggles with forming letters or makes repeated mistakes, we do not put them in time-out, compare them to others, or instruct them to *stop doing it wrong*. Instead, we scaffold, model and support with encouragement. Put simply, we believe in the possibilities of the child. Yet when it comes to behaviour, our approach can shift towards deficit thinking. Mistakes in learning behaviours can be seen as personal failings or intentional defiance. When we enable children the space to get it wrong without correcting or shaming them (even if unintentionally), they then can practice different ways of behaving and self-regulating. So, if a child cannot yet 'behave' ... *we teach*!

Block three: *Regulation is a lifelong process, not a developmental outcome ...*

Kerry recently delivered some training to a group of Early Years educators on self-regulation. At the start of the session, she shared the Early Years Foundation Stage (EYFS) Early Learning Goal for Self-Regulation (DfE, 2025, p. 12). By age five, it is expected that children should be able to:

- Show an understanding of their own feelings and those of others and begin to regulate their behaviour accordingly [as though this is a fully conscious process].
- Set and work towards simple goals, being able to wait for what they want and control their immediate impulses when appropriate [who gets to decide when is appropriate?].
- Give focused attention to what the teacher says, responding appropriately even when engaged in activity, and show an ability to follow instructions involving several ideas or actions [when was self-regulation about compliance?].

As a group, we unpicked how problematic this goal is for children. One of the most glaringly obvious issues with this goal of self-regulation is that it appears to only focus on the ways in which a child complies to the expectation of another which has very little to do with actual self-regulation. This goal amounts to emotional suppression to meet the demands of another. But what made us most uncomfortable is the idea that self-regulation could be seen as an entirely independent developmental goal as opposed to an ongoing and dynamic process. To suggest that we can teach and tick off this important developmental experience underestimates the complexity of networked regulation and overlooks the diversity of human experience – that is, we do not all experience or access regulation in the same way.

While we must teach and co-create skills of self-regulation to equip a child to be able to face their lived experiences in a healthy way, we do not want to suggest that once you have conquered self-regulation that it is a tick-box skill but requires a cradle to the grave mentality.

Block four: *You can't regulate sensations and emotions if you are not allowed to experience them ...*

A reoccurring theme across this book is that, as early educators, we have often been faced with behaviour management approaches that are rooted in stopping, shaping or suppressing the behaviours we find undesirable, challenging and unacceptable. Traditional notions of discipline or the idea that children should be seen and not heard still show up loudly in our education system today. Children's emotions and behaviours can be confronting because they are often quite raw, embodied and unpredictable. We may want to stop them because it is difficult to see a child in distress or we may find them confusing or bewildering. We may also feel pressure that children experiencing and demonstrating human emotions somehow looks like 'bad practice'. This natural urge to stop a behaviour through 'calm downs' or 'don't crys' or with distractions are often with good intentions, but if a child detects that complex emotions are not accommodated, they may learn to suppress or conceal how they might be feeling. Now here is the kicker. If children are not enabled to feel the full spectrum of emotions, they lose opportunities to understand those emotions, how they show up in the body and, most importantly, how to support themselves when encountering these emotional rhythms. The key for educators is to create both space and containment for the emotions that may feel too big for one little mind and body to carry (Butler, 2024) so that a child can safely explore and navigate these, eventually developing a repertoire of techniques and strategies to cope, maintain and thrive.

Block five: *Behaviour gives us information and clues ...*

We have had countless conversations about the ways in which behaviour can be frustrating to support, especially if we do not understand what might be happening for a child. One of the shifts that we made in our own practice is to see behaviour as giving us information and indicators as to what might be happening. For example, I was recently supporting a child who was prone to meltdowns when overstimulated. I noticed that when she was stressed, she would fold into herself, almost like a hedgehog. I could see straight away that this was both a protective response and a way of blocking out the input. The worst thing I could have done in that moment was to physically intervene or to ask her lots of questions. So I respected her hedgehog pose and I focused on reducing stimulus in the environment, such as reducing lighting, moving obvious visual noise and reducing sound input. I gave her space to unfurl. We have both found the advice to look beyond the behaviour quite unhelpful at times because the behaviour is often a significant source of information and gives us obvious and subtle indicators. We have found this particularly important when supporting children who are non- or minimally speaking. It is often the actual behaviour that provides us with crucial initial information, and this initial information needs to be honoured and respected. The key is not to judge those behaviours or indicators, but to take time to decode and figure them out. (See Chapter 5 for ideas on sense-making behaviours with our *building blocks framework.*)

Block six: *Behaviours don't have to make sense to us right away ...*

Leading on from block five was the realisation for both of us that there are some behaviours that won't make sense to us right away or at all, but that doesn't mean we cannot provide access to co-regulation. We have both supported children who have had adverse childhood experiences and trauma; what we have made peace with is that you do not always pull on the right thread to unravel the need. There may be multiple knots that need to be untangled by different people. For example, the child may need access to therapeutic supports or specialist input. That does not mean all is lost or the behaviour should be overlooked, but we have both found that there are often immense pressures on early educators to find the 'trigger' or cause of every behaviour in short spans of time. We so often see early educators beat themselves up, or feel like failures because an ABC chart has not revealed the cause of a behaviour, or experience shame because they have felt de-skilled by a child whose behaviour is complex. We need to create spaces where educators can sit in that place of unknowing without feeling the pressures to have it all figured out. Sometimes our presence is what is needed, not our fix or solution. (See Chapter 5 for ideas on sense-making behaviours with our *building blocks framework.*)

Block seven: *Behaviour can be self-advocacy and rightful resistance ...*

I always share an anecdote when training; it is of a teacher speaking terribly to a child and the child responding to the teacher 'Who do you think you are talking to?' and then being sent to time-out for being rude. Afterwards, I spoke with the teacher and explained that, in that situation, the child was right to self-advocate. He had a right to stand up for himself from the evident adultism (the idea that children are less than adults leading to mistreatment of children). I had enough trust with this teacher for them to take my feedback on board and to think about how they spoke to children. But this example illustrates the wider point that behaviour is a valid form of self-advocacy; as humans we often draw upon our troublemaker behaviours for the greater good. When a child passionately says '*No!*' to a demand, we are usually thinking two things: first, that we might need to support that child in pro-socially expressing their consent or lack thereof; and, second, whether the 'no' is a rightful form of resistance. For example, if someone said to a child 'It is time to stop playing', it is likely they might get 'no' as an answer because play is important to the child. The key for these little acts of advocacy and resistance are teachable moments that can potentially serve the child for life. This point particularly resonates with adult educators who can identify in themselves a tendency to 'people please' – comply and fawn to others – all because they had an education themselves of being told what to do. If you ask us, we think there needs to be more celebration of 'naughty' and resistant children; we need to create safe conditions for all children to be able to explore their own boundaries. (See Chapter 2 for ideas on how to support self-advocacy and rightful resistance.)

Block eight: *We all deserve access to regulation, rest and repair ...*

We often speak to educators who talk of the exhaustion of being an Early Years educator. The end of day emotional collapse of lending your own nervous system to multiple children drains your battery. This doesn't make you a bad educator, it makes you a human one with only so much capacity for all the different rhythms of regulation. Equally, learning behaviour and developing self-regulation as a child is also exhausting (especially if it operates on the wrong assumptions of compliance). The world can be very exhilarating and joyful for the child, but it can also be totally overwhelming. As you will discover as you work your way through this book, regulation cannot happen without access to a range of energy states including rest, flow and alert states. So much of our education system is built on productivity, compliance and calm. A big shift in understanding behaviour comes from seeing regulation through the lens of energy, emotions, relationships and sensory experiences.

References

Butler, S. (2024) *Polyvagal Theory in the Classroom: A Guide to Empower Educators and Support Dysregulated Children and Young People*. Routledge. https://doi.org/10.4324/9781003396574

Department for Education (DfE) (2025) *Early Years Foundation Stage Profile Handbook*. www.gov.uk/government/publications/early-years-foundation-stage-profile-handbook

Neaum, S. (2021) *What Comes Before Phonics?* Sage.

Rypple (2021) Tom Herner, 1998. Available at: https://rypple.org.au/tom-herner-1998/ (Accessed: 27 April 2026).

1 Knocking down the 'behaviour management' blocks

Deconstructing behaviour management

Where did we ever get the crazy idea that in order to make children do better, first we have to make them feel worse?

Nelsen, 2011, p. 14

> **Provocation: The wall**
>
> Imagine standing in front of a large wall. Each brick is labelled with a behaviour you find undesirable or challenging. For example, one brick might say 'shouting', or another 'running off'. Others read 'ignoring instructions', fidgeting', 'hitting others for no reason'. The wall of behaviours is the only thing you can see, and it becomes a barrier to seeing what might lie beyond the wall. The bricks in front of you are what most compete for your attention; all your energy is focused on stopping each of the behaviours.

Children's externalised behaviours

There are three considerations we can explore when it comes to children's externalised behaviours.

Consideration one: When we focus only on the behaviour, it blocks our view and may distort our understanding

Over time this situation can feel exhausting as you cannot seem to see what is happening beyond the wall. But then you start to remove the bricks one by one. At first, you can only see through the gaps, but as you keep thinking about what might be beyond the wall, the bricks start to dislodge with ease. You begin to see a clearer view beyond the wall. This doesn't mean that those bricks are not useful still – remember, they give us that important initial information. Rather, you see the child and their needs, stressors, sensory experiences, relational dynamics, developmental pathways and environmental pressures that were hidden when *all* you could see was the wall.

Brick by brick, as the wall comes down, the child becomes visible again, no longer hidden behind the behaviours that once dominated your view.

Consideration two: Sometimes the behaviour becomes a barrier because of where we choose to stand

There is another consideration too. Sometimes the wall in front of us (the wall labelled with the behaviours you find undesirable or challenging) is one we have inadvertently chosen to stand directly in front of. We stare at it, convinced that we cannot move beyond it, but the wall is freestanding meaning we can choose to walk around it.

Walking around the wall might mean letting go of long-held assumptions about what a behaviour means. For example, the child who seems to hit out for 'no reason' has lots of reasons. It might mean choosing not to interpret a child's actions through a deficit lens. It might mean recognising that some behaviours only become 'problems' because of the expectations we place upon them. When we shift our stance, new understanding becomes possible. We walk around the wall and can see the unmet needs, developmental considerations and regulation states.

Consideration three: Often, the behaviour is the regulation

The third consideration is that we frequently judge behaviour as misbehaviour when, in fact, the behaviour itself is the child's regulation. For example, a child swinging their legs during circle time might be told off for 'kicking', when in reality the movement is helping them stay regulated, focused, or engaged. What looks like misbehaviour is often a child doing exactly what they need to maintain their energy and regulation states.

This book will invite you to deconstruct current approaches and understandings of behaviour and to build new ways of thinking that are more attuned, humanising and developmentally informed. To do this, we first need to examine the origins of how behaviour has been addressed in schooling and Early Years, and how these histories continue to influence our everyday practices. It is time to knock down the walls.

Behaviours can dominate our attention in the Early Years because they often feel like barriers we cannot move beyond. Which behaviours feel like barriers for you right now? Consider noting them down and returning to them later to see whether their meaning shifts as you work through the book.

Introduction

I was recently watching an episode of Educating Yorkshire (2025), a TV programme that offers a glimpse into the lives, education and experiences of children and teachers in a secondary school. In the opening credits, a revealing soundbite is played where a teacher says something along the lines of 'Life would be so much easier working in a school if there were no students.' This immediately set the tone for a season that, to me, visibly demonstrated how dehumanising education has become for children even in the presence of caring educators. Throughout the episode there was an ever-present sense of adultism which can be defined as *the belief, attitude or practice that adults are inherently more important, more knowledgeable or more entitled to power than children*, even in spaces that are quite literally designed for them. I had no doubt watching this show that the teachers deeply cared for and had the best intentions for the children, but I could also recognise that systemically when we operate in systems of control and compliance, we can become complicit in the very harms we are actively seeking to avoid. In several scenes, children could be observed desperately seeking ways to self-regulate, whether that be walking around corridors, looking out of windows, seeking comedic relief, kicking their legs or talking back. And while, there were some wonderful examples of collective and co-regulation through dialogue with invested teachers, most behaviours were viewed through a deficit lens where children were expected to be conformist, docile and fawning to the adults' expectations. While this TV show is for entertainment purposes and there will be many schools that opt for much more relational practices, it raises questions generally on how behaviour is still perceived, dealt with and managed in schools. By extension, in the Early Years there are increasing pressures to ready children for a school system that needs them to fit in and to be malleable to measurement and standardisation. There is also a much deeper conversation to be had about the ways in which teachers and educators are being pushed to the brink of crowd control because of a general undervaluing of those who choose to teach and care for children. This is all to say, we didn't necessarily judge the teachers in this show … rather it raised questions about how the system functions when it comes to supporting children's behaviours.

You may be reading this and thinking that my judgement on teachers is harsh, especially given what they have endured in the last several years, including a global pandemic which has no doubt influenced social and emotional development and the constantly shifting landscape of socio-political and cultural factors. You might even think that I am anti-teacher or unsympathetic to the challenges encountered when trying to educate the modern child. However, my critique of a television show (which also extends to my general issue with the education system) is this: despite the guidance, the policy approaches, the behaviour *tsars*, the evidence-bases and the professional developments, behaviour is getting worse. So rather than being anti-teacher, I am anti the system that is making educators and children feel worse and therefore responding to that feeling with their behaviours. I feel that teachers and Early Years educators are consistently let down by outdated behaviour management (BM) practices. While those of us in the Early Years might like to think we are not exposed or dictated to by behaviour management in schools, the trickledown effect is undeniable as we face relenting pressures to create 'good' children who are constantly calm and regulated. But human development is simply more complex.

We started this book off with three considerations, but now let's move towards a useful quote: 'insanity is doing the same thing over and over again and expecting different results' (Brown, 1983, p. 68). We must break the habit of behaviour management for schools and for Early Years education, de-schooling ourselves, if you will, from practices that quash children's opportunities for genuine collective, co- and self-regulated states. To do this, we must de-tangle behaviour management to explore new possibilities.

What have schools got to do with behaviour in Early Years?

Most schools operate within blanket behaviour management policies shaped by the government's definition of 'good' behaviour, which privileges compliance through systems of externalised praise, reward and punishment, framed as sanctions (DfE, 2024). These approaches are focused on maintaining safety for all children through social order and desirable learning behaviours (which is an important consideration). However, the guidance assumes a universal idea of self-regulation and behavioural control and provides minimal guidance on developmental, contextual and ecological experiences – for example, neurodivergence, disability, social mobility and racialised experiences. Why does this matter for those of working in early childhood and not subject to this guidance? When children transition from Early Years environments, where regulation is usually more relational, responsive and scaffolded, there can be a distinct culture shock for a child who may be used to quality time, talking things through, access to play, choice and reasoning. A fracture exists between early childhood education and primary education in this country where we are working on entirely different operating systems and then wondering why transitions and lived experiences are so difficult for children. Furthermore, we face pressures to get children ready for their schooling experience including an expectation that they are ready to regulate so that they can be universally educated. For many children, this shift can feel punitive rather than supportive, especially if they do not know why the expectations placed upon them have changed quite dramatically thus increasing the risk of exclusionary pathways. For example, research in recent years suggests that children under six are increasingly being excluded from education with behaviour as the main cited reason (Chance UK,

2024). There is only so long that we can blame the children for this behaviour before we have to start looking at the system in which these children exist. That system is behaviour management.

Defining behaviourism before behaviour management

If you are an Early Years educator or teacher, you will be more than familiar with the term 'behaviour management', which is a longstanding and outdated approach to *dealing* with children's behaviours underpinned by a theory known as behaviourism (Skinner, 1953; Watson, 1913). It is built on the surface-level premise that to maintain order requires the identification of observable behaviours deemed acceptable or unacceptable, with desired behaviours reinforced and those considered undesirable reshaped, typically through systems of reward and sanction (you may hear this framed as punishment or consequences also). Behaviourism has very little interest in what might be happening below the surface for a person and is rooted in ensuring that behaviours conform to the social norms and expectations.

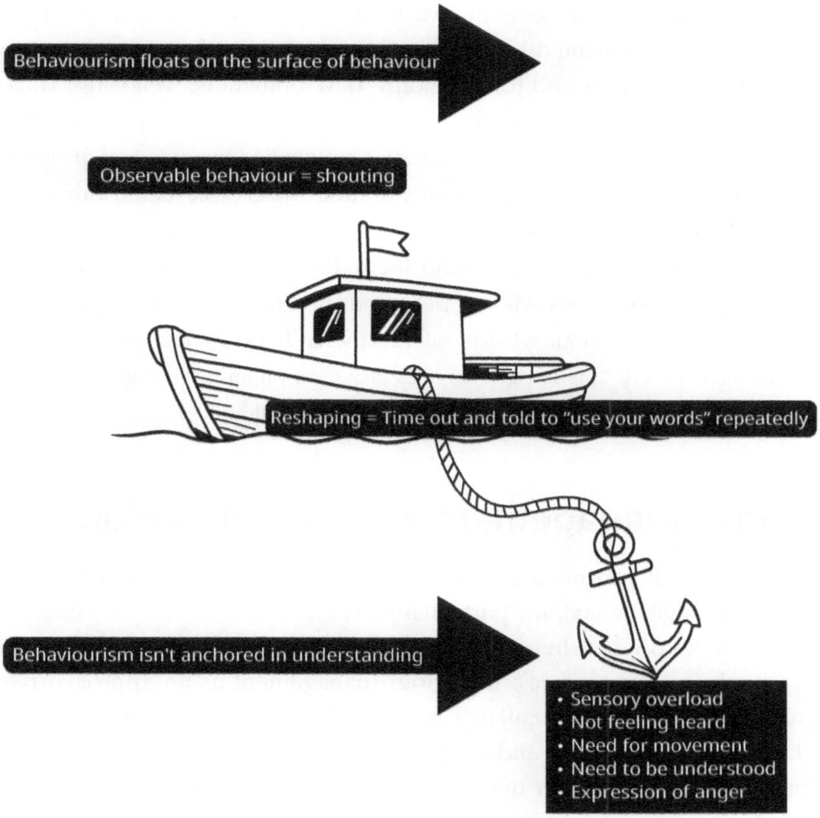

Figure 1.1 Behaviourism in action

You might be reading this and thinking, 'Maintaining order is good though, right?' For example, educators will often say to us that their behavioural expectations are based on getting children ready for the 'real world' (more on this later). And yes … to a degree. We need a level of social harmony and boundaries to be able to exist with and alongside others. However, we also need to recognise that an over-emphasis on order can come at the expense of individual needs and wellbeing; we might all conform to social order, but our feelings of invisibility regarding our needs and wellbeing can mount up – we can end up feeling and doing worse as a result. I often describe it as a row of dominoes. While behaviourism appears to be standing strong, it only takes one domino to fall for the whole row to fall with it.

This is not to say that we should not address or reason with children about their behaviours. For example, when this perspective is shared, educators often raise questions about behaviours they perceive as low-level or easily resolved – for example, if a child needs to be reminded to listen when being given instructions (which is an entirely reasonable expectation). There can be an underlying anxiety that if behaviourism is critiqued too strongly, any use of its methods risks being framed as harmful, leaving educators feeling judged or positioned as intentionally causing harm.

This discomfort does not emerge in a vacuum. Behaviourism, as a theory translated into practice, has a documented history of causing significant harm, particularly when applied rigidly or without regard for autonomy, development or wellbeing. Thus there can be a particular sensitivity about it in marginalised communities – for example, those who are autistic. The legacy of approaches such as *applied behavioural analysis* highlights how compliance-driven models can prioritise observable behaviour over lived experience, contributing to trauma and long-term distress (Aldred, 2025). However, in teaching children about the world around them, there will be times where we must explore pro-social expectations without behaviourism and how to navigate differences while having boundaries about what is safe and what is not. What we do not want to do in this book is to say 'this is right' or 'this is wrong'; again, we want to come back to what is in the best interests and experiences of the child.

Behaviour management in early education

It makes sense that if you need to cultivate behaviours for learning, you might end up trying to manage behaviour, particularly when there are lots of children. The reason it can be so popular in early childhood settings and school is because it can appear to work (on the surface). Behaviour management as an approach refers to 'efforts to control, modify, or regulate one's own behaviour and/or the behaviour of others through social learning and adaptation' (Maguire et al., 2010, n.p.). Some of the original intent of behaviour management was to teach children how to manage their *own* feelings and behaviours, including their thought processes, regulating their emotions and having control over their bodies. Despite the original intent being about teaching a child to have command of themselves, it has long been subject to a power imbalance where it has become the adult that manages, modifies and controls. One of the unfortunate issues that has emerged out of behaviour management is the belief that, as educators, our role is to stop behaviours, rather than to understand them. When the focus is on simply stopping behaviour, there can be numerous consequences for the child including:

- learning to excessively suppress, conceal or mask feelings, emotions and behaviours believing they are shameful and unacceptable (Gross and Cassidy, 2019);
- acting out even more to advocate for themselves (Ijaz et al., 2024);
- neglecting important individual human needs in order to meet the needs of the setting or school (Moore, 2022).

In short, outdated behaviour management focuses on stopping 'undesirable' behaviours without helping children understand their emotions or how those feelings connect to their actions. Without this, it becomes very difficult to equip the child with the lifelong skills that are so often required to thrive and adapt.

Manage and discipline model

The reason behaviour management can be so appealing is it entices us into thinking that the key to solving children's behaviour is to just find the right set of strategies and approaches. For overworked, under-resourced and overwhelmed early educators, this can be turned to, not because it is particularly inspiring but because it might save some of the energy reserves required to do the role. Armstrong (2017) refers to this as *manage and discipline* model, which consists of the following ideas:

- *quantify to control*: behaviour is something that can be quantified and then controlled – for example, all instances of biting can be controlled by the same set of strategies;
- *shape behaviour*: children's behaviour needs to be shaped and managed to meet standardised expectations – for example, all children must follow the 'golden rules';
- *universal training*: given the right training, educators should be able to have complete technical control over all behaviours – for example, having blanket strategies will support all behaviours;
- *exclusion*: children who do not respond to this control are a threat to the orderly environment, rather than the conditions of that environment being incompatible with a difference in behaviour.

(Adapted from Armstrong, 2017)

When we apply this manage and model approach, we end up using crowd control or universal strategies. We can also end up separating the behaviour from the curriculum, thinking it is something that disrupts our everyday practice rather than being part and parcel of early childhood development. So, despite behaviour management priming us to think it reduces our workload, it ends up extending it as we do the same things repeatedly with little resolve.

Put it into practice: Stop yourself before stopping the child

Ensure you stop yourself before stopping the child. A great piece of advice we were given is that when we are observing behaviour we might deem as unacceptable, our impulses can take charge and we predict a misbehaviour. Taking a long pause or deep breaths when you observe behaviours can give your brain and body a moment to catch up and assess the situation. In some cases, you might find it is not misbehaviour but play, or it is a conflict, but the children are figuring it out.

Features of behaviour management

Something myself and Sarah speak about often is that if we went into an early childhood classroom today, we can't say for certain that we wouldn't use behaviour management at times. Anyone at the end of a ten-hour shift can lose the bandwidth and resort to a crowd control technique or lose their capacity to think so deeply about a child's behaviour. And so, as we share these features of behaviour management, we are also asking you to think about when and where they may show up and whether there could be a pattern to why we might return to management techniques.

Activity 1.1 Features of behaviour management

For each of the features of behaviour management here (with examples), consider: *Where and when does this show up in my practice?*

- Feature: The child is viewed as the 'problem'.
- Example: 'Hattie's behaviour is ruining other children's experiences.'

- Feature: The child is deemed to be in control or is making a choice to engage in the behaviour.
- Example: 'Jamel is intentionally hurting other children.'

- Feature: Creates culture of negative labelling.
- Example: 'We call Tarek "Jaws" because he is always biting other children.'

- Feature: Believes that behaviour should be 'fixed' or stopped without understanding why the behaviour is occurring.
- Example: 'Lizzie needs to be trained out of her behaviour.'

- Feature: Reward-, consequence-, sanction- and punishment-driven.
- Example: 'We are ignoring the child and have asked other staff to ignore her when they come into the room because her behaviour is unacceptable.'

- Feature: Adult knows best mentality without providing reasoning.
- Example: 'The child needs to do as they are told because I said so.'

- Feature: Expects quick turn-around in behaviour.
- Example: 'If we put the child on time-out, it should stop within the next few weeks once they have had time to think about their actions.'

- Feature: Is exclusionary and often bias towards marginalised groups, such as neurodivergent and disabled children.
- Example: 'Eugene is autistic and waves his hands during circle time despite being told to use his whole-body listening rules.'

- Feature: Creates a power struggle.
- Example: 'The children should not question my decisions.'

- Feature: Singling out.
- Example: 'No one will want to play with you if you keep behaving this way.'

- Feature: Creates feelings of shame.
- Example: 'You are a naughty child.'

(Adapted from Ruef et al., 1998)

Why behaviour management falls short

When we view behaviour simply as something that needs to be controlled or stopped, our focus shifts to compliance. It is likely to make us more agitated because children are generally not compliant, they are seeking freedom within safe parameters. It can also lead to strategies that miss the mark – for example, aiming to eliminate behaviours we see as undesirable or inappropriate, but failing to address the felt experiences beneath them. When we stay at the surface of compliance, we miss opportunities to teach a child about the repertoire of regulation states they can access. Behaviour management will have short-term gains and, in some cases, if it is a low-level behaviour, it may stop, but we also need to have time to attune to behaviours that suggest an underlying need. So, if not behaviour management, then what?

Behaviour blueprints (old to new way of thinking)

Old blueprint: Behaviour as something to stop

'I need to stop this behaviour.'

When we observe a behaviour that makes us uncomfortable or activates our stress, we can focus too much on simply stopping the behaviour. In some cases, you may need to rightly do this due to a safety factor, but in other scenarios, stopping the behaviour doesn't necessarily address the actual behaviour.

New blueprint: Behaviour as something to understand and resolve

'I need to make sense of this behaviour.'

When we rebuild our thinking, behaviour becomes a source of information. Instead of focusing on stopping it, we focus on making sense of it contextually – for example, are there unmet needs, stressors, sensory experiences, off-balance emotional states, relational dynamics or might it be developmental? The focus should be on meeting or satisfying needs which may more meaningfully resolve the behaviour.

Behaviour scaffolding: Language

Only focusing on the externalised behaviour is one issue, but something else you might want to also consider is the language we might use to describe behaviour, often leaning more towards deficit based or judgemental language. Behaviour specialist, Jen Foster (2023) refers to the 'vocabulary spring clean' when thinking about language, and she highlights that it is important we do this because language can lead to outdated practices and beliefs. By engaging with discussions about language, it also offers us an opportunity to shift our mindset and to essentially ensure that we are moving with the times. Consider the following and how you might re-frame.

Table 1.1 Language shifts

Instead of:	Try this:	Why?
'Lashing out'	Expressing anger	It helps us to recognise that the behaviour is an expression of an emotion or unmet need
Negative reinforcements such as 'no' and 'stop that'	Let's start Try this Do this instead	Using language to scaffold towards pro-social behaviour. Negative reinforcement can escalate or increase stress behaviours.

Instead of:	Try this:	Why?
The child is intentionally behaving this way	The child has some top-down understanding	While children may behave with intention, it is rarely malicious and is more part of their pro-social learning. Using top-down and bottom-up language helps you to think about where they might need support
'Use your words'	I am here for you, show me, tell me when you are ready	During stress responses, children have top-down switch-off, making it difficult to use spoken language
Misbehaving for no reason	I don't yet know the reason	All behaviours have an underlying need or motivating factor, but we just haven't yet figured this out (and in some cases, we might never know)
The child is impacting other children	The behaviour is unsettling for the group or environment	We should be mindful not to stigmatise the child who is experiencing stress and misbehaviour. The impact might be felt by all, and this may be unsettling. The other consideration is that if other children are misbehaving based on one child, it might be that they also have a similar need and so are following the lead of the child. For example, 'A child keeps getting up during circle time and moving around, meaning other children get up as well; this is disruptive.' In this scenario, it is the expression of one child's needs which has highlighted the whole-group need; the circle time should be adapted to incorporate more movement

Rebuilding knowledge: Why behaviour attunement?

While the word 'behaviour' can sometimes overshadow the deeper 'why?', ignoring children's actions entirely would prevent us from recognising the signals and clues that prompt further exploration. In short, we do not recommend avoiding the term 'behaviour', but we do advise against making judgements on behaviour alone without first exploring the underlying needs.

Defining behaviour attunement

Behaviour attunement refers to the recognition that a child's actions serve as the first signal that something deeper might be going on, whether it be an unmet need, a form of communication, an energy state or a sign of stress. By acknowledging the behaviour, educators can take the time to tune in to what might be happening for the child. Sometimes this happens in the moment, while in other cases it may involve ongoing exploration to fully understand the child's experience.

Activity 1.2 Features of behaviour attunement

For each of the features of attunement here (with examples), consider: *where and when does this show up in my practice?*

- Feature: Focused on equipping and upskilling educators to be responsive to behaviour and the underlying experiences.
- Example: 'I am going to provide some visuals for the child to communicate needs to help resolve biting.'

- Feature: Re-frames behaviour and seeks to understand the underlying function, stressor or need.
- Example: 'I can see the child is distressed by the sensory environment and this is translating to their behaviour.'

- Feature: Adopts sustainable strategies that are underpinned by social and emotional wellbeing and welldoing.
- Example: 'The child responds well to having a space to retreat to and rest. I am going to ensure this is available daily.'

- Feature: Acknowledges that behavioural support (and regulation) can take time to embed but it doesn't mean it is not working.
- Example: 'We have agreed with the parents that it may take some months to see the behaviour resolved and we have provided advice and strategies.'

- Feature: Inclusive of all children, and flexible to meet a diverse range of needs.
- Example: 'We provide the child with sensory soothers during group time to help with emotional regulation.'

(Adapted from Ruef et al., 1998)

Why attunement aligns with early childhood development

One of the things we often remind early educators of is that early childhood education is quite literally the space where children come to learn how to behave, regulate and develop socially and emotionally. Therefore, the expectation that all misbehaviour can be quickly eradicated or suppressed defeats the purpose of education because learning is about practice and mistake-making. If we think back to the principles of behaviour attunement (see p. XX), you will remember that we emphasised the importance of seeing behaviour (and regulation) as something you teach. We often hear learning referred to as a journey; as the adult, you have already walked these paths time and time again. Through your guidance, the child can navigate different landscapes of learning which will include many different terrains and pathways. It can be a powerful and rewarding journey for both the child and the adult, but it is not one that is always straightforward. There may be behaviours that are frustrating or uncomfortable to us, and we may find ourselves stressed by the 'ongoing-ness' of some behaviours. That does not cancel out the fact that behaviour is still something that needs to be taught, though we do need to make space for educators to process some of the trickier moments. We apply this logic to other areas of learning, but do not always afford it to children when it comes to behaviour. For example, we would not send a child to time-out if they were not yet able to write their name, nor would we suggest that their friends won't want to play with them because they cannot yet climb up the climbing frame. And yet, those methods are utilised when a child hasn't yet figured out how to tell someone they are not ready to share, or that another child is in their personal space. When myself and Sarah talk about attunement, the thing we come back to time and time again is that it is rooted in compassion to know that emotions, feelings, sensations, energy levels and social interactions are all so difficult to navigate; attunement is about giving children a break from constant scrutiny and judgement. As adults we often communicate to our trusted people, our 'co-regulators', that in times of stress, anger and uncertainty we don't always want a quick fix, what we are seeking is presence, being heard and acknowledged.

Sometimes the best way to attune to behaviour is to read into what it might be telling you about the child.

Behaviour as learning in action

Below are examples of what we might find when we tune into behaviour as learning in action:

- *Testing out ideas*: Child A decides she wants Child B's toy but is unsure what to do about it. She hits the child and takes the toy and is then able to play with it. If unsupported, the testing out of hitting to get something has worked.
- *Exploring boundaries*: There is an open space in the indoor environment and the child begins to run and climb before being told that it is not safe to do so, but the practitioner is more than happy to go outside, or make some partitioning so that other children know it's a movement zone.
- *Giving things a go*: A non-speaking child wants to access a toy that is out of reach and jumps up to grab it. This does not work, so they climb upon a chair to get the toy. The child is not yet able to make a verbal request, so the practitioner reminds the child to use their 'help' visual and sign in future.
- *Making mistakes*: A child engaging in a task that an adult would usually be responsible for because of curiosity, or breaking things.
- *Choosing their own way to do things*: Being resistant to circle time, and sitting still for a long time, as this does not meet their learning needs or interests.

- *Bouncing back*: Child A falls out with Child B and, after taking some time away, realises they would like to re-engage. They approach the Child B cautiously, and are unsure what to do, so they make their physical presence known. An adult provides 'rupture and repair' support and suggests they talk about what happened.

But what about unsafe behaviours?

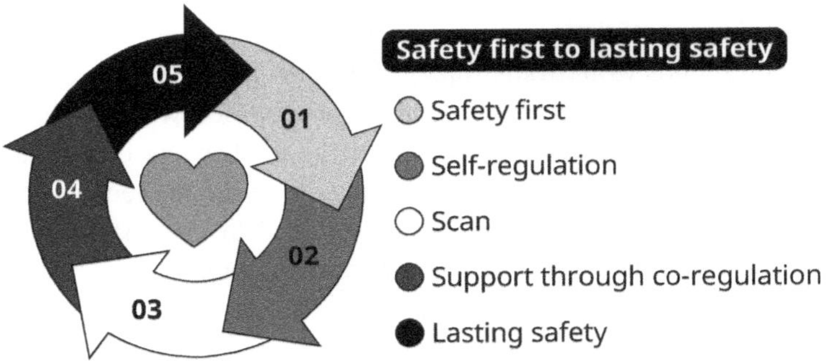

Figure 1.2 A cycle showing safety first to lasting safety

In truth, I think this is an anxiety both myself and Sarah grapple with daily when advising on behaviour. We hear of very high-intensity behaviours – what others might refer to as aggressive or violent behaviour. We have to balance the fact that we do not believe applying the latter terms to two-, three- and four-year-olds is beneficial with finding ways to support them, while also wanting to validate that the behaviours we see from a child of any age can be disorientating. In this book, we refrain from blanket advice or strategies for children we do not know or into whose context we would have little insight. However, we agree that there needs to be better support in early childhood for the diversity of behaviours that fall into the high-intensity category (i.e. hitting, self-injurious, destruction of property etc.). We provide signposts at the end of the chapter, but we also want to draw your attention to a framework for thinking when supporting behaviours that do not feel safe.

The *safety first to lasting safety* approach offers a pathway for responding to children's behaviours through a lens of regulation rather than control. It begins with safety first and recognises that in some scenarios you have to prioritise safety to then be able to access regulation. Our duty of care requires us to act quickly to prevent harm. Once safety is secured, we turn to our own self-regulation, recognising that we cannot co-regulate or collectively regulate if we are dysregulated ourselves. With a steadier internal state, we then scan the environment and consider whether aspects of the space are escalating or supporting the child. This leads into support through co-regulation, where our responses are personalised to the child's internal, relational, external, transitional and sensorial needs (we will address this further at different points throughout the book). The reason we advise this approach is that we know ultimately a child needs felt safety to be able to work through things that are making them feel so out of control; through repeated attuned and consistent responses, they can build the foundations for lasting safety. Over time, they come to recognise their own regulation patterns and begin to use autonomous strategies that support their wellbeing. This approach is not a linear checklist but a cycle that educators move through moment by moment, ensuring that they have a plan in place for high-intensity behaviours that can destabilise the moment. Table 1.2 gives an example.

Table 1.2 Safety First to Lasting Safety

Approach	Need	Lasting safety example
Safety first	With any behaviour, you have a duty to keep a child safe; this is non-negotiable. In these moments, you may need to react quickly to ensure safety is maintained	A child attempts to smack another child, and you place your arm out as a barrier A child is at risk of banging their head during a meltdown and you place a cushion below them and stay nearby
Self-regulation	To be able to support a child, we first need to balance our own scales of self-regulation. The educator must attempt to address their own dysregulation to be able to offer meaningful support	Taking a few deep breaths before approaching a child Registering your emotions and bodily sensations and naming them to tame them
Scan	The environment plays a significant role in escalating or regulating behaviour. Educators should conduct a quick environmental scan and make adaptations as necessary	A child with flight response benefits from accessing fresh air, with obstructions moved out of the way A child with fight response benefits from space to move
Support through co-regulation	Self-regulation is unique to each child; our co-regulation response will need to be personalised and adapted to individual differences and needs	One child responds well to hugs when dysregulated whereas another child would prefer to nest and retreat away
Lasting safety	Where a child is receiving consistent co-regulation, support and being empowered to utilise their own self-regulation, lasting safety will be possible	A child knows how to seek help when dysregulated A child can make autonomous choices to support themselves when dysregulated

Put it into practice: High-intensity behaviours

Make a list of those behaviours that you would consider high intensity, where safety may need to be prioritised. Agree an approach or response so that you have a back-up plan in place rather than reacting in the moment.

Intersectionality insight: What does racialised identity have to do with behaviour?

> I began to notice that when a Black child had big, bodied play, it would be described with charged language such as 'aggressive' and 'boisterous'. Yet, when it was a white counterpart, the language would shift, and the child's behaviours would be described developmentally, such as 'energetic' and 'passionate'.
>
> (Educator reflection)

Despite behaviour management approaches often being advocated as universal and deemed to set standards and expectations for children in a fair way, behaviour management can be anything but fair. There are many arguments that it can lead to discriminatory practices and result in longer-term risks for suspension and exclusion, particularly for those children racialised as Black (Wesley and Ellis, 2017). Implicit bias, which involves involuntary actions and unconscious thoughts influencing educators' decisions, is said to occur when making judgements on a child's behaviour. For example, a study by the Yale Child Study Center (Gilliam et al., 2016) examined implicit bias in preschool educators and found that when primed with scenarios, teachers gazed more closely and for extended periods at Black boys compared to other students, indicating the expectation of disruptive behaviour. This suggests that young Black boys may not be misbehaving more than their peers but rather are being caught misbehaving more frequently because they are watched more closely. Furthermore, teachers' beliefs that Black males were less innocent, more mature and most likely to be perpetrators of misbehaviour contributed to the use of exclusionary discipline against Black boys. This inequitable targeting results in Black children's experiences of early education being impacted by the 'white gaze' and tendency for surveillance. It can be uncomfortable if you are a white or white-passing educator to confront that your judgement of children may differ based on race, but given how this translates to wider society, we also have opportunities to disrupt these practices and enable Black children to show up more fully and to have early experiences of felt safety in diverse spaces where whiteness is not positioned as the dominant norm.

Put it into practice: Bias check

A bias check is a responsible practice. For example, choose one moment tomorrow to pause and ask, 'Would I describe this behaviour the same way if this were a different child?' This simple check disrupts unconscious bias and moves your practice towards fairer, more equitable interpretations.

Conclusion

To be an Early Years educator is a privilege and a huge responsibility. It is a complex role and its complexity is often poorly understood. Across this chapter, we have attempted to outline why behaviour management is an ill-fitting approach, for both children and early educators. It limits us and leads to incomplete understandings of children. By deconstructing behaviour management in its current structure, we can open up our understanding of behaviour being linked to a complex and nuanced human experience. When we rely on behaviour management approaches it can push us into urgency mode – and a deep sense of pressure to resolve or stop behaviours immediately. Our success, however, is not measured by how quickly we can stop a behaviour, but by how effectively we help a child understand themselves so that they go on to develop a wide repertoire of self-regulation strategies.

Behaviour management as an approach is becoming increasingly controversial in the Early Years because it promotes the traditional view that children are 'adults in training' rather than recognising that the social and emotional stages of early development are unique, important and foundational for long-term wellbeing. Behaviour support therefore requires a shift in language, practice and mindset. In our book, we refer to behaviour attunement because we do not believe that behaviour itself can be avoided, overlooked or simply looked beyond; instead we see it as something that helps us to contextualise children's experiences and to find compatible regulation approaches that provide a springboard for children to thrive.

References

Aldred, K.L. (2025) Positive Behaviour Support: discovery, reflection and radical rethinking. *Neurodiverse Connection*, 27 May. Available at: https://ndconnection.co.uk/blog/pbs-discovery-reflection-rethinking (Accessed: 27 April 2026).

Armstrong, D. (2017) Addressing the wicked problem of behaviour in schools. *International Journal of Inclusive Education*, 25(8), 976–92. https://doi.org/10.1080/13603116.2019.1597183

Brown, R.M. (1983) *Sudden Death*. Bantam.

Chance UK (2024) *Too Young to Leave Behind: The Long-term Negative Impact of Exclusions and Suspensions in Primary School (Executive Summary)*. www.chanceuk.com/wp-content/uploads/2024/04/Too-Young-to-Leave-Behind-exec-summary_FINAL-3.pdf

Department for Education (DfE) (2024) *Behaviour in Schools: Advice for Headteachers and School Staff* (updated 19 February 2024). www.gov.uk/government/publications/behaviour-in-schools--2

Educating Yorkshire (2025) Channel 4.

Foster, J. (2023) *Behaviour: The Lost Modules*. Sage.

Gilliam, W.S., Maupin, A.N., Reyes, C.R., Accavitti, M. and Shic, F. (2016) *Do Early Educators' Implicit Biases Regarding Sex and Race Relate to Behavior Expectations and Recommendations of Preschool Expulsions and Suspensions?* Yale Child Study Center.

Gross, J.T. and Cassidy, J. (2019) Expressive suppression of negative emotions in children and adolescents: theory, data, and a guide for future research. *Developmental Psychology*, 55(9), 1938–52.

Ijaz, S., Nobles, J., Mamluk, L., Dawson, S., Curran, B., Pryor, R., Redwood, S. and Savović, J. (2024) Disciplinary behaviour management strategies in schools and their impact on student psychosocial outcomes: a systematic review. *NIHR Open Research*, 4, Article 13.

Maguire, M., Ball, S. and Braun, A. (2010) Behaviour, classroom management and student 'control': enacting policy in the English secondary school. *International Studies in Sociology of Education*, 20(2), 153–70.

Moore, C. (2022) *Behaviour Management in Schools: Legally, the Playing Field has not been Levelled*. Special Needs Jungle, 26 May. www.specialneedsjungle.com/behaviour-management-schools-legally-playing-field-not-levelled/

Nelsen, J. (2011) *Positive Discipline: The Classic Guide to Helping Children Develop Self-discipline, Responsibility, Cooperation, and Problem-solving Skills*. Ballantine.

Ruef, M., Higgins, C., Glaeser, B. and Patnode, M. (1998) Positive behavioral support: strategies for teachers. *Intervention in School and Clinic*, 34(1), 21–32. https://doi.org/10.1177/105345129803400103

Skinner, B.F. (1953) *Science and Human Behavior*. Macmillan.

Watson, J.B. (1913) Psychology as the behaviorist views it. *Psychological Review*, 20(2), 158–77. https://doi.org/10.1037/h0074428

Wesley, L. and Ellis, A.L. (2017) Exclusionary discipline in preschool: young Black boys' lives matter. *Journal of African American Males in Education*, 8(2), 22–7.

2
The shapes of regulation
Understanding dynamic regulation

It is okay that children's behaviour is going to push our buttons; that doesn't mean we cannot show commitment to supporting it.

David Cahn (childminder at Free to Learn, Leeds)

Provocation: The shape sorter

Imagine being handed a puzzle that requires a selection of shapes. You need squares, circles, triangles, stars and rectangles. But when you begin to complete the puzzle, you realise you have only been given two shapes to work with. One set of squares, labelled 'self-regulation', and one set of circles, labelled 'co-regulation'. These are shapes you recognise and rely on, and you can easily slot them into place. Yet the moment you try to place them into the other shape moulds; they do not fit. It becomes clear you need the whole range of shapes. *There are far more shapes than the ones you have been given.*

Regulation is complex

Self-regulation and co-regulation are two interconnected terms that the majority of early educators will have, at the very least, a basic understanding of. As a theoretical concept, it has translated and embedded deeply into our early childhood pedagogies and rightly so. They inform how we understand the complex interactions that unfold when a child feels overwhelmed or swamped by their emotions, sensations and thoughts, and how we, as adults who are assumed to have our own self-regulation figured out, guide and support that child so they feel contained. While we both fundamentally believe in the importance of self-regulation and co-regulation, we are increasingly concerned that these terms are used in catch-all ways. Co-regulation is often stretched to describe both one-to-one interactions and wider-group regulation needs. At the same time, the adult–child interaction is still centred, even when regulation is occurring between adults, or among children themselves. For us, these concepts have become diluted and don't account for the complex network of regulation that is occurring in a setting.

The shape-sorting analogy above is an example of what often happens with self-regulation and co-regulation. We know they are essential, but they are presented in a reductionist way, as though matching one shape to ourselves and one to the child completes the picture. But the puzzle of regulation is much larger. There are many more shapes that influence how children move, feel, recover, connect and learn. Regulation is a dynamic process where we need access to a range of regulation rhythms (or shapes) in order to find the right fit. This chapter intends to guide you in thinking about the different shapes of regulation.

Introduction

Developing regulation skills can be hard and takes time and practice. In our early childhood spaces, children are unconsciously and consciously organising their nervous systems in environments that can be stimulating, exciting, predictable and unpredictable. A common misinterpretation we might make when supporting children is to assume that behaviours are intentional, or a choice. We often coach early educators who will feel a child is consciously choosing to act in ways that the early educator finds unacceptable. As Delahooke (2022) explains, this perspective can lead us to believe that there are acceptable and unacceptable behaviours and we just need to teach children to make better choices – the value of which is defined by us. This approach places an enormous responsibility on the child to act in ways that may be developmentally unrealistic for them. When regulation is reduced to just self-regulation and co-regulation, what should be a reciprocal and relational process that builds emotional capacity can become a transactional set of expectations, where children are required to take on adult-defined ideas of regulation. For example, a child may be feeling angry and want to really act out that anger through movement; we may tell them to 'calm down' or take deep breaths but this may be ill-matched to the sensations of anger.

For Sarah and me, we are passionate that self-regulation and co-regulation are enabled to be more varied and dynamic rather than presented only as universal sets of techniques. To do this, we need to understand the developmental diversity of regulation and how to build strong foundations with enough variation to meet children's emotional blueprints.

Behaviour blueprints (old to new way of thinking)

Old blueprint: Self-regulation means being calm

'Self-regulation means being calm.'

Calm spaces, corners and calm co-regulation can be wonderful and necessary. But sometimes they take priority over the whole spectrum of self-regulatory responses.

I do not want children to be calm (compliant) when we are about to sing action rhymes. I want them energetic and ready to move and use their voices.

I do not want them calm when playing. I want them active, embodied and in a flow state.

My reflection is that calm is necessary but not enough. We need to think about the up and down of self-regulation. And calm will look different for every child. If we think of ways that as adults we try to bring a sense of ease and calm, it will look varied – and often physical – for example, pacing or running … activities not often looked on as calm states in early education.

New blueprint: Self-regulation is a dynamic and fluctuating process

'Self-regulation is a dynamic process where children need to draw on different arousal and relaxation states.'

When we teach and model self-regulation in the context of co-regulation, it is also important children understand that it is more than just managing feelings. It also includes:

- energy accounting for different states;
- accessibility with autonomy (being able to express needs and make choices);
- sensory preferences, attunement and sensitivities;
- communication preferences.

From newborn to now being

None of us is born with the natural ability to regulate and control ourselves independently. In fact, as newborn babies we were entirely driven by our survival instincts. We likely screamed and cried to make our needs and presence known, and we relied on a more knowledgeable other, usually our primary caregiver, to offer familiarity, predictability and safety (Chaves and Taylor, 2020). Our internal world likely felt chaotic and arousing, with feelings of hunger, tiredness, discomfort and other physical sensations. The external world either contributed to that chaos or offered us a state of ease that let us know 'everything is going to mostly be okay' (truthfully, we all probably experienced a combination of both). If we think back to the idea that we were once small babies instinctively looking to find our place in the world, we would each have a unique map of memories, experiences, locations and layouts that have shaped who we have become since being newborns. Many of us can trace the experiences that strengthened us and the experiences that weakened us without seeing the physical evidence of it in our brains. However, our minds and bodies carry their own 'intelligence' letting us know how we are likely to respond to experiences. Think of the times your gut instinct kicks in to let you know your feelings about something (Aldred and Aldred, 2023). We might think of this as embodied regulation, recognising that our experiences of the world are felt from our head to the tips of our toes, and that we cannot separate our brains from our bodies. Whether you care for and educate babies, ten-year-olds or 21-year-olds, understanding regulation as an ongoing practice across the lifespan offers important insights into just how dynamic it is, and how crucial it is to human flourishing. Put simply, this is not a solo journey, but one shaped through the communities we exist within, where collective experiences can sit alongside and honour diversity.

If regulation is ongoing and informed by prior experiences, then early childhood education holds both a responsibility and a privilege. This means honouring regulation as a process by offering children repeated opportunities for positive experiences, while also providing sensitive scaffolding during moments of challenge. To do this, we need to understand the different types of regulation and how they might be accessed.

The definition and dynamics of regulation

How might we define 'regulation'?

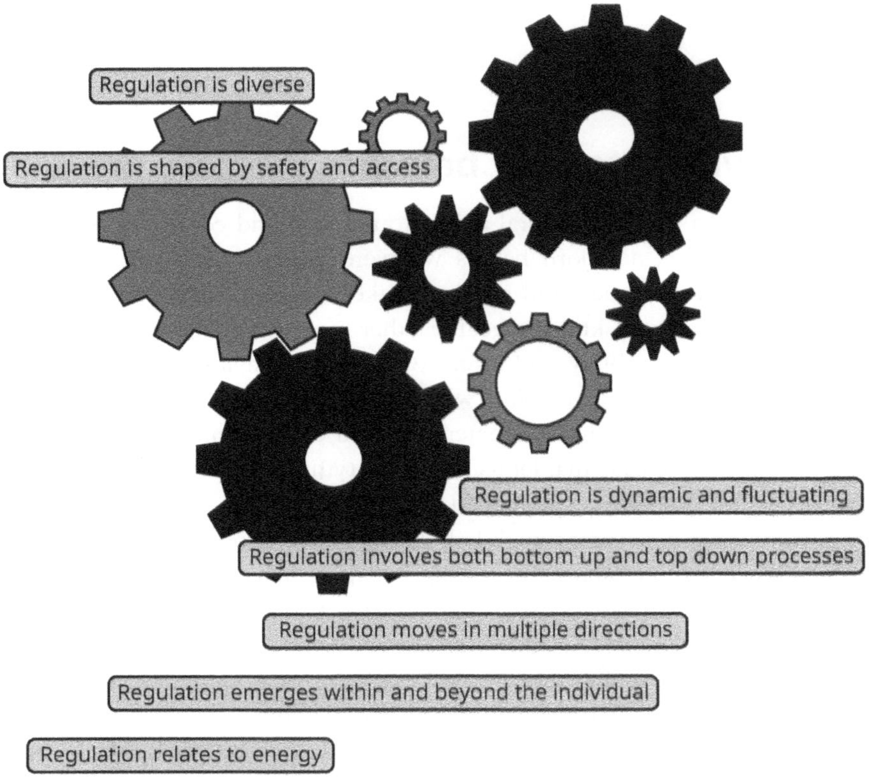

Figure 2.1 Dynamic of regulation

One: Regulation is diverse

We explored lots of definitions of regulation through the lens of education and one of the discomforts we encountered is that it can often present as quite a *silo* definition. For example, we read one definition that suggested regulation is the ability to modify emotions and respond to situations with balance, calm and control. In fact, there are lots of definitions that amount to a person essentially being able to control themselves and to respond to everything in a calm manner. To us, this only tells one part of a story.

Two: Regulation is shaped by safety and access

As we worked through our thinking on regulation for this book, we found ourselves returning repeatedly to the same tension. Scientific definitions offer useful structure, but they are not enough on their own. We also wanted to ground regulation in lived, relational and embodied experience. This tension pushed us to look within and beyond dominant psychological models of regulation, and to ask whose experiences these definitions were built around and whose they might exclude.

Given the emphasis in research to focus on control in self-regulation, we reflected on our own interpretation of regulation. We spoke a lot more about the need to feel safe when emoting and to not be shamed in our expressions of regulation which can be so varied (Corbyn and Aldred, 2025). We also explored the work of Mullan (2025), who looks at emotions through a decolonised perspective (rejecting dominant narratives) in which she recognises that humans are learning to safely tolerate activating thoughts, feelings, emotions, energy states and sensations without feeling overwhelmed by them. When that overwhelm is not threatening (or when it is shared by another), it is possible to choose a response that matches. However, safety itself is a privilege and there are many structural factors that might make it harder for a child to access co-regulation and self-regulation. For example, if a child is experiencing discrimination or adversity such as exposure to racism, ableism or poverty, safety to access regulation can be compromised. This is important for an early educator to consider when developing regulation practices in their setting to both recognise that regulation is not a one size fits all and to assume some responsibility for breaking down barriers to feeling safe. To do this, we must consider regulation as a dynamic process.

Three: Regulation is dynamic and fluctuating

Dynamic regulation describes the ongoing, fluid process of safely moving between different emotional, sensory and energy states throughout the day while being able to maintain relative *ease* between shifts. It recognises that regulation is not a single state like calm, but a dynamic rhythm shaped by relationships, environments, sensory

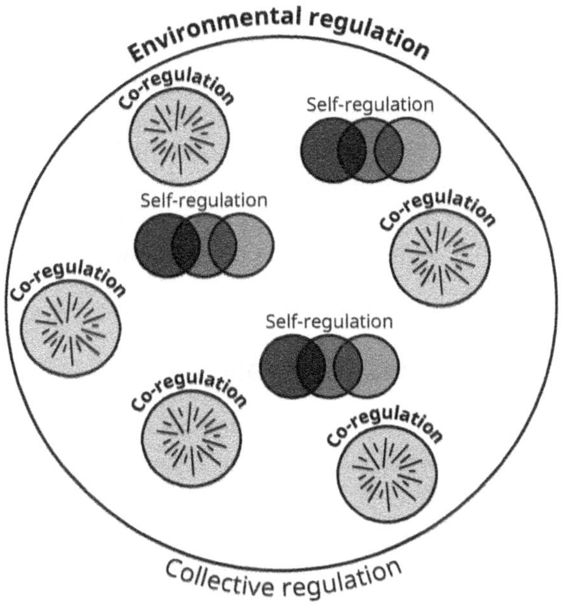

Figure 2.2 Regulation states

experiences and internal cues. *Children do not and should not be trained to stay in one state.* This is not co-regulation and can sometimes lead to coercion or crowd control. Children's regulation rhythms rise, dip, spark, pause, recharge and re-engage. Dynamic regulation honours this natural oscillation and supports children to move between states safely and authentically, rather than pushing them towards one preferred state.

Dynamic regulation develops when children are given plentiful opportunities to have different regulation states activated. For this to happen, they need to be in environments where they can emote without shame (Corbyn and Aldred, 2025). Regulation might be noticeable through embodied or unruly behaviours, different play frequencies, diverse interactions, active learning, critical thinking and questioning, desire for autonomy and rest.

Dynamic regulation also recognises that there will be times when collective regulation is needed to ensure safety of the group or to reserve the bandwidth of the adults – because you are actively regulating too. In short, as educators we simply cannot be constantly co-regulating individual needs without thinking of the community.

The shapes of regulation

The shapes of regulation help us identify the different sources and supports that children draw on to regulate. These shapes do not operate in isolation. They interact constantly, shaped by context, relationships and capacity.

Self-regulation

Self-regulation is a child's unconscious and conscious capacity to find equilibrium between their behaviours, emotions, energy states and sensory experiences by drawing on a repertoire of right-fit responses. It develops through relational scaffolding and modelling and should be understood as a lifelong dynamic experience rather than a developmental milestone. Self-regulation includes regulating up, regulating down and moving into flow states.

Co-regulation

Co-regulation is the responsive and attuned support an adult or peer provides to help a child organise their response to a behaviour, emotion, sensory experience or energy state when demands exceed their current capacity. It is the relational foundation that makes self-regulation possible.

Collective regulation

Collective regulation describes how groups, communities or classrooms shape and share emotional, sensory, energy and behavioural rhythms, helping each other feel safe, steady and connected. It recognises that regulation is not an individual task, but something that emerges through shared routines, interactions and culture.

Environmental regulation

Environmental regulation refers to the ways the physical, social, temporal and emotional space helps balance children's sensory needs, emotional cues, energy rhythms and behavioural demands through predictable design, accessible materials and rest and rise opportunities. The environment acts as a regulating springboard that reduces stressors and offers right-fit cues for engagement.

Protective regulation

Protective regulation refers to the ways a child might respond in order to keep themselves safe in moments of threat, overwhelm, or reduced capacity. Often described as dysregulation, these responses are not a failure to regulate, but an attempt to maintain safety; however, they may be mistaken as misbehaviour. Protective regulation may look intense, abrupt, or socially challenging, yet it serves a clear function for the individual at that moment.

Put it into practice: Access to regulation

Using the regulation shapes to guide you, think about how you might provide access to regulation across the day and within your setting. You might think about how to build strong foundation and access, but how you might also consider variations?

Activity 2.1 Co-regulation or collective regulation?

This activity invites you to reflect on everyday moments in early childhood settings and consider whether they are better understood as co-regulation or collective regulation. The aim is not to find a single correct answer, but to notice how regulation is shared, distributed and shaped through relationships, routines and environments.

Read through the list of everyday situations below. For each example, decide whether you see it primarily as *co-regulation, collective regulation*, or a *blend of both*. As you decide, reflect on *why*. Consider who is doing the regulating, who is benefiting and how regulation is being supported. Discuss your reflections with a colleague, or jot down notes about how these moments show up in your own setting.

- An adult sits beside a distressed child, matching their breathing and offering quiet reassurance.
- The whole group sings a familiar song to support a transition between activities.
- A practitioner lowers their voice and slows their movements during tidy-up time, and the room gradually settles.
- Children copy one another's movements during an energetic outdoor game.
- An adult adjusts the lighting and noise level in the room after noticing rising agitation across the group.
- A child leans into a peer during story time for comfort.
- The group follows a predictable routine with some rules that help everyone know what is coming next.
- An adult supports one child to step away from the group when things feel overwhelming.
- Children laugh together during shared messy play, becoming more animated and engaged.
- A practitioner offers a hand squeeze or shared rhythm to help a child through a difficult moment.

Many moments in early childhood settings do not sit neatly in one category. Regulation often moves between co-regulation and collective regulation, reminding us that it is relational, shared and shaped by context. If you would like to review how we defined each of these moments, please refer to the Co-regulation and collective regulation chart at the back of the book on page XX.

Four: Regulation involves both bottom-up and top-down processes

When we are born, our nervous system develops sequentially meaning that experiences, skills and capacities are acquired over time, with our brain's greatest priority being survival in order to develop. There are functions required in our brains that are necessary for life, including being able to breath, sleep and digest food (to name a few). These functions are involuntary and automatic meaning we don't necessarily consciously think about them, although it is important over time to become aware of these autonomic functions and to understand that humans need to care for one another to regulate these functions, such as rocking a tired infant to sleep. The reason we provide care for infants and young children across the lifespan is because we know that, without it, it would be impossible for a child to survive. In short – a caregiver acts as a buffer to provide the foundations for the other sequential phases of brain development to occur.

Examples of bottom-up influenced behaviours

- A child is sat playing with their cars and another child enters their personal space suddenly leading to the child to hit out (fight response).
- A key person stands over a child and looks down at them with an angry face leading to the child to run off (flight response).
- A child screams when they are told repeatedly to stop being silly and their name is said with a negative intonation (fight response).
- There are lots of children in one space with lots of noise and the child hides (flight response).
- A change in routine leads to the child shouting 'no' repeatedly and swinging their body in protest (fight).
- Another child is screaming leading to the child also bursting into tears and screaming (fight).

Examples of top-down behaviours

- A child answers back asking why there is a rule or expectation in place (development of reasoning).
- A child hits out at a friend, but then apologises when she realises she has upset her friend (bottom-up and activation of top-down).
- A child says says no and expresses their dislikes (advocating).
- A child talks about their angry response by explaining their bodily sensations (interoceptive and emotional awareness).
- A child is told off for talking, but points out 'other children are talking too' (reasoning).
- A child says they feel angry and begins to do deep breathing (interoceptive and emotional awareness).

Five: Regulation moves in different directions

If you imagine an average day in your early childhood setting, you are likely to encounter children regulating in many ways. Some children may seek rest and quiet in the book corner after a busy lunchtime, while others may need to run off the energy that has built up from sitting for a prolonged period. From early in life, we begin to develop some capacity to notice what our bodies are telling us we need, and to try out different responses to see what helps.

This process is closely linked to our sensory system known as *interoception*, our internal body sense, which communicates through sensations how we are feeling and what we might need (Hoyle and Hyde, 2024). For example, a sensation of fullness in our belly after lunch may lead us to choose to lie down with a book in a quieter space. Over time, growing interoceptive awareness allows us to respond more automatically to our needs. These sensations become predictive, giving us time to act.

A very familiar example is the sensation of needing to go to the toilet. Without this internal signal that need could arrive suddenly and without warning. Interoception buys us time, not only for our basic physical needs, but also for our emotional ones. For instance, the sensation of fear can prompt decisions that help keep us safe, such as avoiding poorly lit or isolated areas. The bodily sensations of fear, combined with emotional and cognitive responses, may also lead us to change our pace or behaviour to move out of that state more quickly.

What we are illustrating here is that regulation mobilises us into different responses, and this is usually demonstrated through the idea of regulating up and down, along with maintaining our regulation state.

Regulating up

Regulating up occurs when the child's energy is too low, flat or depleted. They may appear withdrawn, sleepy, immobilised or slow to engage. These states reflect the body's attempt to conserve energy, often after stress or high demand. Regulating up offers the gentle boost needed to reawaken alertness and readiness. Movement, rhythm, warmth, music, novelty and co-regulated interaction can all help build energy gradually, without overwhelming the child.

Maintaining regulation

Maintaining regulation refers to supporting a child to remain within a state that feels steady, engaged and manageable for them. The aim is not to hold a child in stillness or calm, but to protect access to a state where they can participate, connect and learn without tipping into overload or depletion. This may involve small, responsive adjustments such as predictable routines, relational check-ins, access to movement, sensory supports or moments of pause. Maintaining regulation recognises that staying regulated requires ongoing environmental and relational support, and that this state is dynamic rather than fixed.

Regulating down

Regulating down happens when the body has built up too much stress or activation and needs to return to a state that feels safe, steady and manageable. A child may show this through overwhelm, agitation or intensity. Regulating down supports the body to decrease activation and find calm. Children often need sensory gentleness, predictable routines, relational reassurance and opportunities to slow their pace. This is not about making a child compliant. It is about restoring balance so that their nervous system can recover.

Six: Regulation is accessed from within and beyond

What we are essentially suggesting in this chapter is that regulation comes from within, but it is also accessed outside ourselves, whether that be from another person or the environment. If the child does not yet have capacity or is unable to access regulation in that moment, they can borrow from elsewhere and the key is that there are plenty of opportunities to borrow so that the child can succeed.

Behaviour scaffolding : Mapping the shapes of dynamic regulation

To help you move from the narrow bi-directional view of regulation to a more dynamic understanding, let's explore how the dynamic shapes of regulation show up in your own context. Look at the questions below and note down the ways in which you support dynamic regulation across your setting:

- self-regulation (what options do children have to access self-regulation in your environment?);
- co-regulation (what types of co-regulation do educators utilise or draw upon in everyday practice and how is time made for this?);
- collective regulation (what techniques and approaches does your setting utilise for collective experiences of regulation?);
- environmental regulation (how is your environment designed for access to dynamic regulation?).

(You may find that more shapes emerge as you work. That is part of the learning.)

Prompts

- Where do snacks, movement breaks or quiet corners sit?
- What happens during transitions?
- How do adults offer support when a child is overwhelmed?
- How does the space itself do some of the regulatory work?

Reflection questions

- Which shapes of regulation do I rely on most?
- Where might children be expected to do the hardest work alone?
- Where is the environment carrying the load, and where is it not?
- Whose nervous systems are being most accommodated here?
- Which children might struggle in a system shaped this way?

Needs not naughtiness

A really important aspect of regulation is that it helps us recognise when a need is present. Over the last decade, there has been a deliberate shift away from the idea that children misbehave for no reason. While the word 'naughty' is used less often in modern education, children's behaviour is still frequently framed in ways that imply wrongdoing, rather than signalling unmet needs. Adopting a needs-based approach to regulation helps us move beyond judgement and towards understanding, enabling us to respond in ways that genuinely support a child's regulatory needs.

A very common framework referred to when thinking about children's needs is *Maslow's hierarchy of needs*. We have long held reservations about this hierarchy and have found ourselves weary at how often it is referred to without necessarily effectively shifting practice. The hierarchy proposes that we must fulfil needs in a sequential order to achieve self-actualisation, but this approach is not effective for all children. The reality is that needs do not always need to be met sequentially. Instead, we can adopt a *balancing system* approach where meeting enough needs can help create an equilibrium. This approach recognises that the needs of children can be complex and multifaceted, and meeting some needs may not necessarily lead to the fulfilment of others. Thus, a balanced approach that considers individual needs can better accommodate more personalised support for the diverse needs of children.

The *existence, relatedness, growth* (ERG) theory of needs is a psychological framework proposed by Clayton Alderfer as an alternative to Abraham Maslow's hierarchy of needs. The three elements represent the three core categories of human needs identified in this theory.

1 *Existence needs*: This category encompasses the basic material and physiological needs required for survival, similar to Maslow's physiological and safety needs. It includes the need for food, water, shelter, safety and physical wellbeing.
2 *Relatedness needs*: Relatedness needs refer to the desire for interpersonal relationships, social connections and a sense of belonging. This category encompasses the need for love, affection, friendship and positive social interactions.
3 *Growth needs*: The growth needs category encompasses the desire for personal development, self-esteem, achievement and self-actualisation. It aligns with Maslow's esteem and self-actualisation needs. These needs are driven by an individual's desire to grow, learn, develop skills and achieve their full potential.

According to the ERG theory, these three categories of needs are not strictly hierarchical or sequential, as proposed in Maslow's theory. Instead, individuals can experience multiple needs simultaneously and if one need is not satisfied they may shift their focus to another need category. This concept is known as the *frustration-regression principle*. For example, if growth needs are not met, an individual might regress to pursuing relatedness or existence needs.

The ERG theory also acknowledges the concept of frustration and satisfaction. Frustration occurs when a higher-level need is blocked or cannot be fulfilled, leading individuals to focus on lower-level needs. Conversely, satisfaction arises when needs are met or fulfilled, promoting psychological wellbeing and motivating individuals to strive for further growth.

Overall, the ERG theory provides a more flexible and nuanced perspective on human needs, recognising that individuals can have multiple needs simultaneously and that the frustration-regression principle can influence their motivation and behaviour.

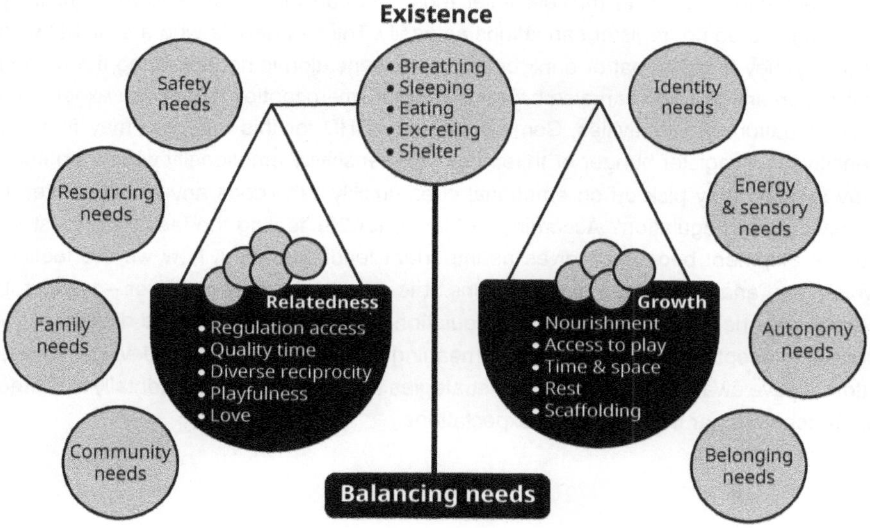

Figure 2.3 Balancing needs

Intersectionality insight: Our nervous systems

One of the reasons we have both felt uncomfortable with how self-regulation is taught in Early Years is that it works on the presumption that all our nervous systems are essentially susceptible to the same things. But the reality is that while we know everyone benefits from safety, relational support and connection, our nervous systems do not all develop or acquire in the same way. We referred to interoception earlier and return to this idea because it can be a developmentally diverse experience. So, a reminder of what it means.

(Continued)

Interoception is the sensory system that helps us notice and interpret the internal signals of the body. These signals include hunger, thirst, needing the toilet, changes in heart rate, muscle tension and shifts in breathing. Interoception also underpins how we recognise and make sense of our emotional states. When we feel sad, anxious, excited or overwhelmed, our bodies generate corresponding sensations. For many children, especially those with interoceptive differences, these sensations can be difficult to detect, name or connect with specific emotions. This creates challenges in self-regulation because a child cannot respond to needs they do not yet recognise.

Children can experience differences in their sensitivity to interoception. For example, some children may have a heightened sensitivity, meaning they register those sensations at a higher intensity. For example, Kerry is autistic and has heightened interoception and finds the sensation of needing a wee intolerable; this means even a slight detection results in multiple toilet trips. You can also have a lower sensitivity meaning you do not register sensations as easily. Think of people who are ADHD who may say they forget to eat or drink because the sensation is not activating the person into action enough. You can also have paradoxical interoception where you experience a combination of sensitivities. Coming back to ADHD for this one, you may find low sensitivity for register hunger or thirst, but high sensitivity emotionally where a person may suggest they pick up on emotional cues quickly. Why does any of this matter in behaviour and regulation? According to Mahler (2026) 'feeling the feels' is a must for our development because it gives us important feedback about how we are feeling, which then enables us to make decisions. It is a motivator and mobiliser – without it, we can experience disorientating dysregulation. For neurodivergent and disabled children, interoception can be unreliable, meaning we need scaffolds to develop unique interoceptive awareness and adaptive strategies that include developmentally informed approaches rather than universal expectations.

Seven: Regulation relates to energy

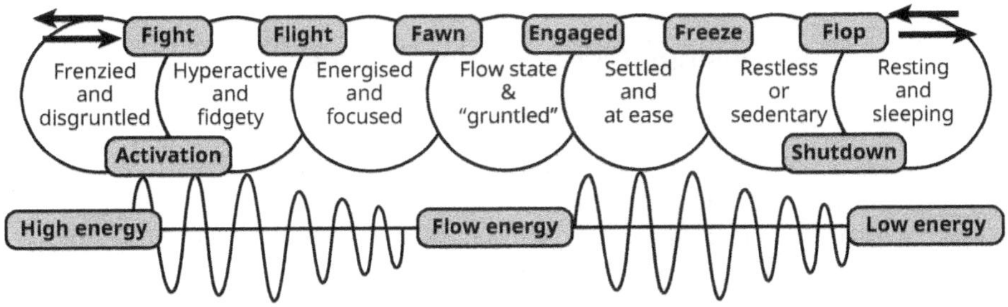

Inspired and adapted from Laurent & Fede, 2019 (update 2022)-Autism Level Up which is Copyrighted and Foster, J. (2025) Classroom Engagement: The Unwritten Code. London: Sage Publications.

Figure 2.4 Energy states

Source: Inspired and adapted from Laurent and Fede (2022) and Foster (2025).

Increasingly, educators are coming to understand regulation as related to the amount of energy you have in your body. Energy regulation can be described as a developmental construct that helps us to understand how energy can translate in our arousal states (Laurent and Fede, 2021). For example, a child might need to draw on high energy when completing a playful obstacle course, leading to high arousal. Similarly, they may look to lower their energy levels to take a nap, leading to low arousal. Our energy states and levels of arousal differ dependent on our developmental profile, meaning that some children might have a good grasp of their energy levels whereas others need support to figure out how to move between arousal states.

When we think about energy states and arousal levels, we also need to consider the role of stress both emerging internally and from external factors such as the environment, relationships and transitions. For example, imagine a child comes into the setting in the morning raring to go with lots of high energy and then they are told they need to sit still in a circle time for 20 minutes using whole-body listening. If that energy has nowhere to go, the level of arousal may be too much to contain, leading to what we might then label as misbehaviour, such as the child kicking out their legs, or shouting out, or distracting others. What we have to ask in these moments is whether the child is misbehaving or if their high energy has been misread and they are now experiencing stressors. You might want to think about what you do in those moments – whether you push for compliance or whether you can read signs of energy, arousal and stress. To do this, let's explore stress responses in the early childhood environment.

The role of stress in regulation

One of the most useful ways of thinking about children's observable behaviours is to consider their different states of arousal. Arousal is defined as 'a state of physiological and mental alertness' (Nicholson et al., 2018, p. 9). We experience arousal for many different reasons, including stress, energy and pleasure. There is understood to be an optimal level of arousal where children are self-regulated and can match their energy to the task at hand, but children can also experience too much or too little arousal, leading to a heightened risk of becoming dysregulated (or the scales become tipped out of balance). Arousals can activate the fight, flight or freeze response.

Stress responses

- *Fight*: Experiences a physical surge and reaction and may act or speak out. May feel like being about to spring into attack mode and/or on the defensive – for example, a child swinging their whole body and shouting 'no'.
- *Flight*: Experiencing a need to flee, escape or hide. May feel a sense of urgency and trapped. May engage in avoidance behaviours – for example, a child trying to find their way out of an environment or running away and hiding.

- *Freeze*: Feeling stopped in your tracks. May have difficulty thinking or speaking and might feel 'stuck in the moment'. May appear to have delayed reactions – for example, may stay close to a familiar adult and seem dazed. Freeze can also include disassociation, where risk-taking behaviours occur – for example, running out without an awareness of danger.

Variation behaviours within stress responses

- *Fright*: Becoming hypervigilant and feeling sensitive to threats or perceived danger. May feel highly reactive or sensitive to physical, environmental or sensory stimuli – for example, a child may seem jumpy and unsettled.
- *Fawn*: Becoming overly compliant and masking usual behaviours to fit in. May shift boundaries or people-please to avoid demands or judgements. May feel scared to say what they are thinking or feeling – for example, a child going along with an activity or experience to please the adult.
- *Flop*: Experiencing mental collapse or a tendency to feel unwell and unsteady. May feel nauseous or report being unwell – for example, a child saying that their tummy hurts.
- *Flood*: Experiencing a flood of emotions, struggling to distinguish between energy states, sensations and emotions and how these might translate into feelings – for example, a child shifting between moods quite rapidly as they try to organise the sensations within their body and the thoughts running through their head.
- *Fixate*: Experiencing a rumination on a particular thing, such as running the same thing repeatedly through the mind and not being able to break the cycle – for example, a child fixating on a child snatching their toy and feeling the situation is unresolved.
- *Resist*: Experiencing resistance or avoidance of perceived demands and actively going against expectations (sometimes justified) – for example, a child refusing to join in as they still feel affronted by a situation or do not think it makes sense.

Case study: A freeze response?

I was recently in an early education setting where a child appeared to be experiencing a clear freeze response. She seemed to be in shutdown. When spoken to, she could not respond verbally. Her posture was very still and upright, and she remained rooted to the spot. Despite this, several adults continued trying to get her to move. For around ten minutes, they talked at her, repeated instructions and enforced expectations to relocate. When this did not work, they approached another educator to intervene.

He walked over and positioned himself directly in front of her, so she was staring at his midriff while he spoke down to her. His tone was relatively friendly, but his commands were firm. 'You need to come with me to the other space, or I am going to have to move you because it is not safe to leave you here.' I was visiting the setting and knew that intervening in that moment would risk escalating the situation further. I could also feel my own stress rising as I watched a group of adults who were not yet able to recognise the signs of a stress response or adapt their approach to match what the child's nervous system needed.

The reality was that this child was not refusing to comply. She was not making a choice. She was not in a position to come with him, make a decision or respond to reasoning. Every ounce of her energy was going into managing the stress inside her body. What perplexed me most was that the adults had an easy alternative available. They could have simply made the space safe and said something like, 'We can give you some time.' A hands-off approach would have been the most attuned and least intrusive response.

- How do I recognise the difference between a child choosing not to comply and a child experiencing a stress response such as freeze or shutdown?
- In moments of distress, how does my physical positioning and tone either support or override a child's bodily autonomy?
- What would it look like to slow down, step back and create safety without requiring the child to move, respond or meet my expectation?

Stress is unavoidable

Stress can be positive, tolerable or toxic.

- *Positive*: Brief increases in heart rate and a mild elevation in stress hormone levels. This may be activated by a minor change in routine, working out a problem or trying to navigate peer interactions.
- *Tolerable*: A serious, temporary stress response with increased heart rate, elevation in hormone levels and may last longer than positive stress. Think of it like carrying a residue of stress and it needs to be shaken off. This type of stress is often best buffered by supportive relationships.
- *Toxic*: Prolonged activation of stress response systems which has a physiological, hormonal and cognitive impact. This type of stress cannot just be shaken off, but has a lasting impact on healthy development. There is often an absence of or inconsistency in protective relationships.

Stress and dysregulation

Stress is the body's natural response to a perceived threat or challenge, whether physical, emotional, or psychological. It triggers a 'fight-or-flight' response, causing the release of hormones like cortisol and adrenaline that prepare the body to react to danger.

Dysregulation refers to a child's reduced capacity to regulate their physiological reactions including stress, emotions, feelings and actions. There can be a mismatch among these reactors making it difficult for the child to process, make choices, prohibit impulses and work towards a healthy goal or outcome. For example, imagine a child is subject to lots of transitions in the day and becomes increasingly stressed by the demands and changes. It can be difficult to manage or regulate the amount of stress that is occurring and the child may hit out or cry to indicate that they have an unmet need or prolonged exposure to stress.

Resistance as regulation

I was recently speaking with an educator who explained that she felt some children were being disrespectful. The children she was referring to were two and three years old. We talked about whether children of this age genuinely understand the concept of respect, and whether their behaviours are an attempt to communicate respect to adults. Respect is an abstract and complex idea, and it is also subjective. In other words, there will always be wide variations in how different people understand respect and disrespect.

Together, we explored how this expectation might reveal an over-focus on social rules rather than an understanding that children's behaviours express their current needs, energy states and intentions. A child not following an instruction is not necessarily choosing to ignore it. Often, the behaviour is telling us that something in the interaction, the demand, or the environment is not matching the child's capacity in that moment.

As children grow, this becomes even more important to recognise. A child who is beginning to develop social awareness may not yet understand the social rules expected of them. Their resistance to these rules can be a form of regulation, as well as a signal that the expectations may be incompatible with their developmental profile. For example, when children consistently shout out during group time, the behaviour may be communicating that this part of the routine is not working for them. You may introduce strategies to support turn-taking, but you can also recognise that children need opportunities to speak up, join in, vocalise and move through their communication loops. Their resistance tells us something about their needs; when we listen to it, we are better able to create environments where children can regulate, participate and thrive.

Conclusion

When all that is made available to us is the idea that we must co-regulate in order to teach self-regulation, is it any wonder we come up short time and time again. When we began writing this chapter, we wanted to honour the importance of both self-regulation and co-regulation, but we also wanted to place these experiences within a wider ecology of needs, sensations, relationships and systems. This feels especially important in early education, where you may have a whole room of children with busy, developing nervous systems, and the expectation that to care and teach well, you need to be able to distribute or lend your nervous system in order to better equip self-regulation skills. That is an exhausting role to take on.

It made sense, then, to explore the different shapes of regulation across a busy nursery day, and how these shapes fit together to create dynamic regulation experiences that keep everyone intact – for example, recognising that you will naturally move between co-regulation and collective regulation depending on what is accessible and realistic in that moment, and knowing when to carve out pockets of quality time for deeper co-regulation.

This is never going to be a perfect science because we are messy human beings. But having a repertoire of regulation approaches to draw from offers something far more meaningful and sustainable for both children and adults. And this prepares us for the next chapter where we will think more deeply about your self-regulation.

References

Aldred, K.L. and Aldred, D. (2023) *Embodied Education: Creating Safe Space for Learning, Facilitating and Sharing*. Self-published.

Chaves, J. and Taylor, A. (2020) *The 'Why' Behind Classroom Behaviors, Prek–5: Integrative Strategies for Learning, Regulation, and Relationships*. Corwin Press.

Corbyn, J. and Aldred, K.L. (2025) Beyond mind: the embodied double empathy problem. In D. Milton (Ed.), *The Double Empathy Reader: Exploring Theory, Neurodivergent Lived Experience and Implications for Practice*. Pavilion.

Delahooke, M. (2022) *Brain–Body Parenting: How to Stop Managing Behaviour and Start Raising Joyful, Resilient Kids*. Hachette.

Foster, J. (2025) *Classroom Engagement: The Unwritten Code*. Sage.

Hoyle, A. and Hyde, T. (2024) *Becoming a Sensory Aware School: A Toolkit to Develop a Whole School Approach for Sensory Wellbeing*. Routledge.

Laurent, A.C. and Fede, J. (2021) Leveling up regulatory support through community collaboration. *Perspectives of the ASHA Special Interest Groups*, 6(2), 288–305.

Laurent, A.C. and Fede, J. (2022) *Autism Level Up!* www.autismlevelup.com/

Mahler, K. (2026) *Interoception: Feeling the Feels* [online training series]. https://ocali.org/Interoception-Feeling-the-Feels

Mullan, J. (2023) *Decolonizing Therapy: Oppression, Historical Trauma, and Politicizing Your Practice*. W.W. Norton.

Nicholson, J., Perez, L. and Kurtz, J. (2018) *Trauma-informed Practices for Early Childhood Educators: Relationship-based Approaches that Support Healing and Build Resilience in Young Children*. Routledge.

3

Scaffolding regulation

How adults support regulation

Teachers teach who they are.

Zwolak, 2018

Provocation: Who you are

Imagine an educator and a child. This educator feels that 'time-out' never did them any harm. They keep their feelings to themselves. This is who they are. It informs their practice with young children. The child is different. They wish they had someone to talk to. They have been told that they need to think quietly and individually about what they just did.

'She needs to learn to cope'

When watching a TED talk by Steve Zwolak on the importance of Early Years, a quote that stood out to us was this: 'teachers teach who they are' (Zwolak, 2018). It resonated deeply as I reflected on how I taught and cared for young children early in my career.

As a new educator, I drew heavily on my own experiences of being taught. One of my strongest memories from school was often feeling scared and confused. It was not an easy experience, and yet I internalised it as a template for how I thought children were meant to be taught and cared for. Without realising it, I absorbed the belief that children needed pressure or fear to behave.

I was also a child who needed a lot of closeness, and I grew up hearing that I needed to be more independent or to learn to 'cope'. Early in my practice, I unintentionally repeated that narrative. I remember once saying about a child I was key person for, who had become very attached to me: 'she needs to learn to cope'.

Thankfully, I was surrounded by thoughtful Early Years educators who gently re-routed me. They encouraged reflective practice and guided me towards professional development that helped me unlearn what I had been taught. That support enabled me to rebuild my approach in a way that was more relational, attuned and affirming.

We have to acknowledge, as early educators, that we are only human and that the art of connection and shared regulation does not require us to be perfect or technically precise. Regulation is a complex process with many dynamics at play. Drawing awareness to this, and being willing to share our stories, does not make us 'bad' educators. It makes us conscientious and grounded in the understanding that regulation is built through a network of wisdom, reflection and relational knowledge.

Take a moment to think: what does your teaching teach to children? What might they internalise by the way you teach?

Introduction

We often explore with early educators why they remain committed to early childhood education when we know it is a space and place that can come with many challenges and is a high-demand role. Many talk of the joy and rewards that come from caring for and educating young children, but they also recognise that they often do this within a system that takes its toll. On an average day you are managing multiple spikes in your stress and energy levels and if these go unaddressed they will build up. While minor spikes in stress are expected, such as managing transitions or repeating headcounts to ensure children are safe, there are also more significant stressors that can influence how we show up in our role. There is often a widespread expectation that to be a 'good' educator you must suppress stress or always appear calm and regulated. The difficulty is that suppressed stress has nowhere to go, especially when you are in a role that requires continuous caregiving, responsiveness and emotional availability. Self-regulation and co-regulation are often presented as skills we should simply be able to do, without enough recognition that they are incredibly complex, dynamic and labour-intensive practices. Accessing different regulation states also depends on being part of an early education infrastructure that supports, rather than hinders, our capacity to regulate. This includes an appropriately funded system that provides financial security so educators can remain in their roles, and professional development that is sensitive to the diverse developmental experiences of children. What we are mindful of doing in this book is suggesting that when it is positioned that the burden of care should come down solely to the endless goodwill of early educators who continue to give over and above and just accept that, this will come at the expense of their own mental health. Research suggests that for early educators to maintain good mental health in their role they need professional development opportunities to learn more about their own mental health, and they also need opportunities with others for co-regulation, relational supports and connection (Stein et al., 2022). Hochschild (1983) described this as educators recognising that to manage the *emotional labour* of a caregiving role, it must come with time to engage in *emotion work*. One does not come without the other, yet we know there are significant gaps in focusing on the role of the early educator in terms of mental health.

When we think of stressors on educators, we must also consider the systemic pressures that weigh heavily on the early education sector, with Early Years educators carrying much of this load. While everyday stress may build up, it can be made worse when working in systems that de-value the role of the Early Years educator. Stress is a recurrent theme in this book, but it is important to make clear in this chapter that self-regulation is often presented as the individual responsibility of the educator. It can also often be assumed that as a female-dominated profession, self-regulation already exists within our toolkits as part of our maternal instincts. But the reality is that regulation exists within a network where we will draw on different regulation states based on our own lived experiences and the context in which we exist. While we will explore specific stressors, in the current climate we must also recognise the systemic issues that can impact capacity and the bandwidth for behavioural support, including emotional, sensorial and social development.

Systemic issues impacting educator wellbeing:

- policy and practice
- time deprivation
- compassion fatigue
- underfunding
- self-efficacy
- adult mental health support
- supervision quality
- underfunding
- workload
- lack of resources
- CPD quality
- child factors.

Our way to wellness is not through suppression

Good levels of adult mental health have a direct and positive impact on children's mental health, experiences and outcomes. If we want to prioritise children's wellbeing, then we must also commit to cultivating a culture of wellness for the adults who care for them. This means our workplaces matter. As Moxley importantly states, 'our workplaces should contribute to our wellbeing, not be a risk to it' (n.d.).

Care work also exists on a continuum, shifting between experiences that lift us up and those that weigh us down. At its best, care is reciprocal and fulfilling. It is a partnership that supports the growth of others while offering joy, connection and self-expression. Many educators feel most alive when they can integrate their talents, creativity and relational gifts into their practice. Yet care can also become burdensome when it is reduced to a series of tasks or chores, especially when structural pressures or staffing limitations prevent educators from engaging in the relational aspects of care that bring meaning and balance.

The research base is clear that stress within caregiving environments is not static. Practitioners often have limited capacity to draw on their own self-regulation strategies because, unlike children, they cannot leave the situation when stress escalates. When escape is not possible, the stress response can shift from flight to fight, increasing the likelihood that behaviours escalate on both sides (Ollison, 2019). Stress is also physiologically contagious. Observing or absorbing the stress of others has measurable effects on our own nervous systems (Max Planck Institute for Human Cognitive and Brain Sciences, 2014), meaning that educators may carry the weight of both their own stress and the stress they witness in the children around them.

When adults are supporting children through moments of dysregulation, much of their energy is spent suppressing their own emotional responses in order to remain outwardly calm. This reduces the time and internal space available for tending to their own self-regulation needs (Frivold Kostøl and Cameron, 2020). Over time, this can lead to what has been described as 'empathy switch-off' (Zaki, 2019), where the emotional demands of caregiving become so heavy that the capacity to feel with others diminishes as a protective mechanism.

Taken together, these insights remind us that educator wellbeing is not a luxury or a personal responsibility. It is a structural and relational necessity. If we want adults to be able to co-regulate with children, we must ensure the environments around them are capable of co-regulating with the adults. The emotional labour of early education cannot be sustained on individual resilience alone. It must be held, supported and nourished at every level of the system.

You have to feel it to deal with it

One of the consistent points we make to early educators is that children's behaviours, including the ones we label as misbehaviours, are an inevitable and expected aspect of early childhood development. To exist in an early education space and expect constant compliance is to set yourself up for failure. Children are in our settings to learn how to behave, and this learning unfolds over time as they experience the rhythms of regulation and the full range of feelings that come with being human. The only way to develop an understanding of your emotional and embodied self is to be enabled to experience the range of emotions and feelings without shame, and to have time to figure these out and to organise those feelings. For example, anger can be such an overwhelming feeling for an adult or a child, and to be told that anger is bad and to 'calm down' means that there is a real missed opportunity to sit with the feelings of anger, and to find a tuned in response. In that moment, we can validate that anger is an inevitable emotion and we can teach the child how to process and respond to anger in ways that are safe. We often frame this to early educators as 'time

'time-to' rather than 'time-out' meaning children cannot learn to manage their own emotions and feelings if we are taught to ignore them or other them. We have to find ways to get more comfortable (or at ease) with the uncomfortable expressions.

Behaviour is confronting

One reason we may find it difficult to sit with uncomfortable emotions, feelings and behaviours is that you might never have been taught how to do it. Relational approaches to behaviour ask us not only to support children's emotional experiences, but to notice our own. This can be confronting, particularly when someone else's way of expressing or regulating their emotions sits outside what feels familiar or safe to us. For example, if someone expresses anger through movement, loudness or physical energy, this can feel intimidating to some adults, even though the person may be using movement to regulate. In contrast, someone who expresses anger by talking a lot may feel more manageable or acceptable, depending on our own sensitivities and experiences. What we find tolerable or challenging is shaped by what we have learned, what we have been exposed to, and what we have been allowed to express ourselves.

Many of us grew up with clear messages about 'right' and 'wrong' ways to show emotion or respond to distress. When these messages go unexamined, they can quietly shape how we interpret children's behaviour and what we expect of them. Without reflection, we may project our own discomfort, limits or learned rules onto children, rather than pausing to consider whether those expectations are reasonable, relational or supportive of regulation in that moment.

Put it into practice: Introduce a code-word for de-escalation

If you are in a setting where there are multiple educators, a code-word can be a good strategy for ensuring that you can seek support when your stress levels have peaked. For example, if there is a behaviour that you are struggling to support and you know your regulatory consistency is waning, using a code-word for help needed can be beneficial. Similarly, there are situations we often observe where an educator is engaged in regulation with a child and another adult steps in making the situation worse and leaving the educator frustrated that they were in the thick of the situation and needed time and space. A code-word for 'back off' can also really help.

Behaviour can de-skill us

It is not uncommon for early educators to encounter behaviours that make us feel isolated, de-skilled or resentful. After all, we are meant to be the calm, rational, objective grown-ups who know what to do. And yet behaviour is often ambiguous. We do not always have an immediate read on why something is happening – not only can the behaviour itself be a stressor, but the uncertainty around it can too. When these stressors build up, the pressure to remain calm can feel threatened and we may find ourselves trying to control children rather than connect with them. But what if we pushed back against the idea that a good educator is always calm, always composed and always able to suppress their own emotions? What if we acknowledged that to be effective in regulation we need time, space and permission to engage more deeply with our own complex emotions as we support young children? To do this, we need to develop a deep understanding ourselves in order to connect with others.

Understanding the role of educator stress

Stress is going to show up in your early educator role. It is inevitable and it can be manageable. When we understand the role of stress in the early childhood environment through the lens of the early educator, we can be empowered to create emotional climates where we know that we matter too.

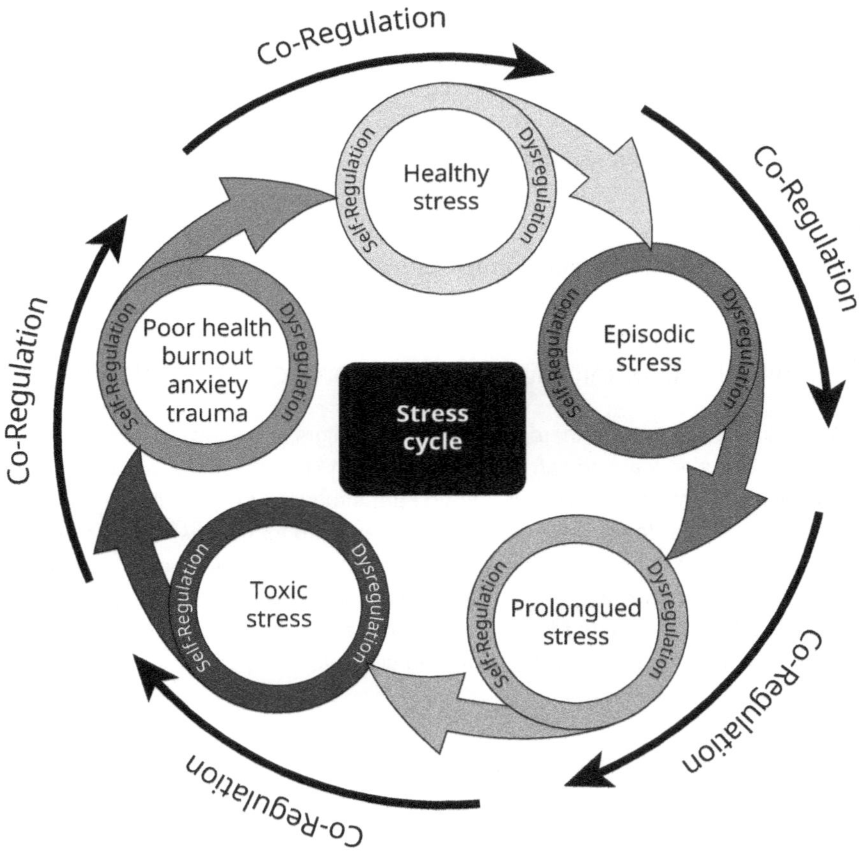

Figure 3.1 Diagram of the stress cycle including stages: healthy, episodic, prolonged, toxic stress and trauma. Arrows indicate co-regulation and self-regulation between stages

What is stress?

In simple terms, stress is how our brain and body react when a threat is detected. It is a biological and innate process that helps us to remain vigilant so that we can react and respond appropriately to real, perceived and 'felt' danger. Healthy stress causes minor physiological changes such as an increase in heart rate and a rise in stress hormone levels (Kesäläinen et al., 2022). For example, if you were driving down the street and you heard the sound of sirens, the sirens would activate your stress response system so that you would know to move out of the way so that the ambulance can pass. From this example, it is clear to see that stress can move us into appropriate action and response, also known as becoming *mobilised*. You might refer to this as healthy or acute stress in that it serves to support you, keep you alert and occurs within a short burst. Once the ambulance has passed, you may take some deep breaths to steady yourself, or recognise that by moving out of the way, you have enabled the ambulance to do its job of supporting people in need. If you translate this to your everyday educator role, your stress response system is what keeps children safe – for example, you may notice a child hovering close to the edge of a tall climbing frame and you may alert the child so they can re-route or you may stand close by in case of a fall. We start here because we do not want any Early Years educator to view stress itself as a bad thing. It's a necessary thing. We also experience stress responses for positive experiences too ... such as in anticipation or excitement. Let's think of the climbing frame again; you may be observing a child climbing great heights for the first time and you feel the surge of adrenaline at seeing them take a risk, but you are also there to catch the fall. This type of stress creates elevations that are manageable and you do not necessarily need lots of time to recover.

For stress to remain healthy and manageable, humans develop the skills and capacities of self-regulation (and co-regulation) so that felt danger can be regulated and maintained without having a detrimental impact on our wellbeing. For example, imagine you are having a busy day at work. The demands from others become overwhelming which activates your acute stress response where you might realise that you feel tired or running low on energy. Your response to the threat of too many demands may be to request your afternoon break where you can self-regulate and to step away from the demands. Again, you have been mobilised into responding to the stressor. However, if you noticed that you regularly feel stressed by ongoing demands, this would be referred to as *episodic stress*, meaning that this type of stress is something you encounter frequently and may be having an impact on your wellbeing.

Stress is a natural response and we can often manage it on our own. However, some stress can last longer or happen more often. When your stress response is frequently activated, it can start to take a toll on your mind and body. For example, if you work in a chaotic environment where you don't feel supported, you may feel constantly overwhelmed, exhausted, or even get sick more often. This happens because your mind and body aren't getting the chance to recover and reset from the stress. Worryingly, research increasingly indicates that the role of the Early Years educator is one which includes prolonged stress because of the instability of the workforce, young children's difficult behaviour and mental health needs, workplace stress, low systemic support and high levels of burnout (Stein et al., 2022). If this prolonged experience of stress goes unsupported it can become *toxic stress*. This type of stress can lead to permanent changes in our brain and body and therefore should not be left unsupported or ignored.

The other consideration for the Early Years educator is that stress does not just come from one place; it comes from many. Sometimes your type of stress can have different origins, but its expression happens in the place you spend most time, unless you are able to suppress it. For example, you may have a stressful personal or home life and this seeps out at work. One of the expressions we often hear in education is that you need to learn to leave your 'baggage at the door', but we find this terrible advice. We need to learn how to safely store our baggage at work so we can do our jobs, but then we should not leave it to accumulate.

So, what does this have to do with children's behaviour? The first thing to mention is that stress is contagious. The second thing to say is that, in the same way that we are on the receiving end of our children's stress, they are on the receiving end of ours. If we do not understand our stress responses or have a way to manage them, children may inadvertently take on the burden of our stress.

Put it into practice: Instead of asking 'What is wrong?', ask 'What has happened?'

Framing your thinking in this way helps you to move on from seeing the child as a problem when supporting behaviour that includes a stress response. You may be thinking about what happened in the immediate moment, or whether the child has developed a stress response from other experiences. This curiosity to understand means that you can then develop truly responsive approaches when supporting young children.

Stress responses

When you experience a stress response, your body will have a preferred way of responding (Aldred and Aldred, 2023). These responses are described in Table 3.1.

Your stress blueprint

One of the key things that we advise early educators to do is to complete a stress blueprint. This enables the early educator to explore their own stress and response experiences so that they can be better prepared for those moments of overwhelm.

Table 3.1 Stress responses

Stress response	Definition	Examples
Fight	The fight response helps us to move into immediate action to resist whatever we perceive as threatening. It is the moment we spring into action and are driven by movement and moods. Core reflexes can take over, meaning all your energy goes to the muscle groups and the brain	Arguing Outbursts Physically responding Irritability
Flight	The flight response helps us to get away from a situation and so we might spring into action, but also try to escape the perceived threat. In this moment, our logic can go 'offline', making it difficult to rationalise what is happening	Wanting to remove yourself from a situation Avoidance or ignoring Hiding Covering ears or face
Freeze	Hypo-freeze or 'flop' is when we become immobilised. It is the moment where we submit to the threat because we cannot see a way out. It can happen when we are in a terror state or experiencing extreme fear	Withdraws or tunes out Loss of interest or motivation Restrictive or repetitive actions Memory issues Fatigue People-pleasing

What we have both found is that when you know your stress triggers you can plan for them and you can consider how you might support yourself. Similarly, we have found that when you are able to talk to your colleagues about the different ways you approach stress you can then also support each other.

Sarah and I will now share an example.

Kerry: When I completed my stress blueprint, I realised that I often have a freeze response when I am stressed. This means I will often go quiet or feel extra lethargic and sluggish. Others might think I am sulking or stonewalling, but I am just preserving energy. One thing that helps me is if I can reduce sensory load, such as lower lighting, access to fresh air or space. I also share with my colleagues that I am less likely to be communicative; if they keep asking me if I feel okay, this can make me feel way worse. The best thing to do is to give me space.

Sarah: My stress blueprint shows that my common response to stress is the fight response. I might appear irritable and this might be uncomfortable for others (and indeed me), but what I am feeling is a need to react now and manage the situation, which is done with good intentions. In that moment I might feel that the onus is on me to immediately act, when in fact what will really help me is to talk it through with a colleague or tune in to what is actually happening in the situation. This helps to let that immediate fight response dissipate a little.

If you want to complete your own stress blueprint, you can access it at www.diversepathways.org, under resources.

Put it into practice: Complete your stress blueprint

There are days when things might feel too much, and your wellbeing may feel impacted. When we feel stressed, it can feel difficult to focus on the small steps to feeling well. Take some time to outline your main wellbeing priorities and ensure that you make time for small joys. These things might not solve all of your problems, but small acts of self-care can be nourishing.

For each of the wellbeing priorities you list, note down a time you will attend to them.

Many people have some awareness of the responses to stress, but less often think about their minds and bodies preferred ways of responding. However, it can be useful to be able to identify your stress responses so that you can better self-regulate or seek co-regulation (yes – adults need co-regulation too).

Put it into practice: Reason to regulate

During a conversation with an Early Years educator, they explained that when they are feeling stressed and out of energy, they tend to lean towards statements such as 'because I said so' and 'because these are the rules'. The questioning from children becomes something she wants to shut down. We talked about the fact that, for her, the repetition was as draining as the questioning and that she may save time by using reason to regulate. If humans can make sense of something, or see the reason for it, they are more likely to follow it, especially if it is in fact logical. So, when we take time to give a clear reason for something, we give children time to make sense, but we also spend less time trying to enforce expectations without explanation. For example, if I am asking children to be quiet, I might say 'could we be quiet for a moment so that everyone has chance to hear the instructions'.

Case study: The origins of a stress response

This example was shared during a training course on behaviour. During the session, we asked Early Years practitioners what their main flashpoints were regarding behaviour. A flashpoint is a behaviour that you find emotionally triggering and therefore may have greater difficulty supporting from a place of compassion and understanding – essentially something that activates the adult's stress response.

The practitioner shared that she absolutely could not abide children who bit and that, in her view, biting was entirely unacceptable, no matter what age the child was. We explored the practitioner's flashpoint of biting during this session and why this particular behaviour created such deep emotional discomfort. Sometimes, the key to working our way through a flashpoint is to connect up the dots as to why it has become a flashpoint in the first place. As we explored her feelings about biting, she suddenly recalled a time when her own child went to nursery, and she explained the following:

> My son started nursery and, on his very first day, I got a call from a practitioner explaining that he had been bitten by another child, and that they wanted to let me know as it had broken the skin. I remember being so consumed with anger that someone had caused such pain to my child. He was so distressed, and it made settling so much harder as he became fearful.

This traumatic experience had remained with the practitioner, and we were able to discuss the origin of those emotions when she supported biting in her own professional role. By connecting the dots and hearing the perspectives and experiences of other colleagues, the practitioner could address some of the discomforts around biting.

Some reflections on this case study:

- flash points often relate back to our own personal experiences or memories, and it is important to be respectful that we each have our own frame of reference for understanding behaviour;
- connecting the dots in flash points is useful because then we can explore ways to navigate our way through and ensure that we provide an equitable and fair response to behavioural concerns;
- exploring flash points as a team or with a colleague can be helpful both to *normalise* sharing and talking about emotionally triggering behaviour and to create a supportive culture where adults' own frame of references, strengths and areas for development are understood.

Our own self-regulation capacities

It is important to take some time to recognise that, as adults, we are also consistently developing our self-regulation capacities. When you think of self-regulation, it is not uncommon to think of the things that make you feel dysregulated – for example, the things that annoy, frustrate you or make you feel emotionally uncomfortable. The reality is that there are a lot of behaviours that are going to push our buttons or make us flip our lids. This is not something to feel shame over, but something to recognise and engage with so that you can resolve why certain behaviours might feel unsettling.

Activity 3.1 What are your flashpoints?

We each will have our own flashpoints when it comes to behaviour.

Think about those behaviours that cause you to have an uncomfortable emotional reaction. List those that you find most frustrating or annoying. We will discuss these shortly.

Side note: it is okay to be entirely honest with yourself here. Part of the way to understand behaviour is to explore some of our uncomfortable feelings surrounding it.

Compassion fatigue in co-regulation

Kerry recently delivered a training session to a large group of Early Years educators. When she came to the section on *compassion fatigue*, she was shocked to realise that not one educator had heard of this experience before, given that early childhood educators work within environments that are sensitive due to the diversity of development and difference. Generally, compassion fatigue refers to an individual's reduced capacity or motivation to be sensitive, empathetic and responsive to another individual's emotional experiences (Chen et al., 2023). It would make sense, then, that if educators are co-regulating children consistently across time, they are at risk of compassion fatigue. And yet it is a largely understudied area in the field of early education. However, compassion fatigue must be taken seriously as the risks associated with it are serious including:

- physical symptoms including exhaustion and headaches;
- heightened stress responses including anger, frustration and sadness;
- absenteeism due to vulnerability to illness;
- emotional experiences including depression and loss of hope.

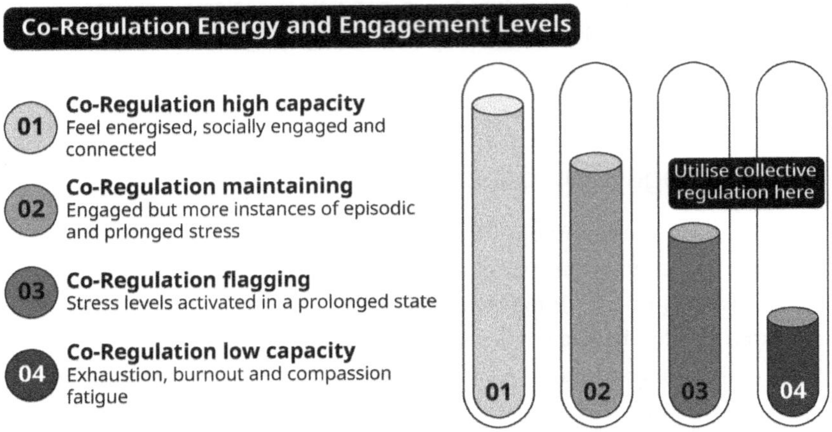

Figure 3.2 Bar graph depicting co-regulation energy and engagement levels with four categories: high capacity, maintaining, flagging and low capacity

Identifying compassion fatigue

Table 3.2 Co-regulation to compassion fatigue continuum

From	To
Power of care	Weakness of care
Joy from giving	Difficulty receiving
Advocating for others – speaking powerfully and honestly	Not speaking up for oneself – passive aggressive language
Putting others first	Lacking self-care
Contributing towards and doing meaningful work	Feeling burned out and underappreciated
Caring in communities and in relationships	Caring causes feelings of isolation
Being empathetic and sensitive to other's perspectives	Taking on emotions of others and taking things personally
Being agreeable and encouraging	Having difficulty saying no
Work is rewarding and purposeful	Feeling indispensable, becoming a workaholic and doing too much
Doing essential work that is the infrastructure of a community	Feeling invisible and at the bottom of a hierarchy
Nurturing others towards autonomy	Creating dependency or suffocating others to try and 'fix' them
Being helpful, cooperative and giving	Lacking boundaries
Feeling capable and self-sufficient	Having difficulty asking for help or delegating

Source: Murray, 2022.

Behaviour blueprints (old to new way of thinking)

Old blueprint: Venting about children's behaviour

'I need to vent about this child's behaviour.'

When we are stressed and we feel we have nowhere to take that stress, it can lead to venting about children's behaviours. On occasion, we meet with early educators who have had such a stress build-up that they speak about children in ways that are not always helpful. We don't judge this; rather we want to understand that when you are not given time to process what is happening, it can turn into frustration.

New blueprint: Processing children's behaviour

'I need time to process and make sense of this child's behaviour.'

An alternative to venting is processing. We need to create spaces for early educators so that they can talk about the things that have made them feel uncomfortable, frustrated and upset without that leading to further labelling or negative perceptions of the child.

(Continued)

Research tells us that when those who work in a caregiving capacity can engage more deeply with their complex emotions, they have lower levels of exhaustion and burnout. And their self-efficacy is increased making role performance stronger (Nicholson et al., 2018).

Venting versus processing

An example of venting:

> 'He was horrible all day today. His parents need to sort it out. There is no excuse for the behaviour. He gets away with so much.'

An example of processing:

> 'I found Harry's behaviour really difficult. It made me feel angry and frustrated. I wonder how he felt too. I think I need to talk it through with someone.'

Intersectionality insights: Spiky profiles and stress

One of the biggest stressors that I encountered as an Early Years educator was that I was expected to be an 'all rounder' in the role. It is something that really concerns me about early education because I do not think humans are generally built this way. We all have strengths, weaknesses, traits and needs and it is about identifying our own holistic profiles so that we can work towards our strengths, and ensure our struggles or weaknesses are appropriately supported. As an autistic and ADHD early educator, I was forever in trouble for not being consistent. I had a sensitive stress system and though I was quite good at supporting behaviour it was usually because I could mask my stress and then I would collapse at the end of the day. It was only when I explored my professional capacity through a *spiky profile* that I was able to better advocate for myself because I was able to show where my distinct strengths lay, but where my capacity may fluctuate. So, what is a spiky profile? This phenomenon describes a pattern in which the gap between strengths and weaknesses is more pronounced than it is for the so-called average person. It is commonly associated with neuro-minorities, including people with neurodevelopmental experiences such as autism, dyslexia and ADHD. When these strengths and challenges are mapped visually, they tend to appear as high peaks and deep troughs, creating what is often described as a spiky profile. In contrast, neurotypical or more conforming individuals are more likely to show a flatter profile, where differences across areas are less pronounced. In practical terms, this means that a person with a spiky profile may stand out in the workplace, not because they lack capability, but because their abilities and support needs are distributed differently.

What is your body budget?

According to Barrett (2020), the brain is often thought of as being primarily responsible for thinking rather than survival. But the main goal of the brain in life is to keep us alive. The way in which it does this is to ensure that our nervous system functions effectively enough through a series of interactions from both within and outside the mind and body. Throughout our day, the brain is continuously engaged in managing both withdrawals and deposits. If we do not effectively tune into this system, we place ourselves at risk of exhaustion and burnout. This system applies to the children, but also to you; it can be a great way of maintaining your wellbeing.

Deposits:

- a good sleep
- nourishment (food, drink and comfort)
- movement
- smooth transitions.

Withdrawals:

- poor nourishment (food, drink and comfort)
- poor sleep
- holding in emotions
- stressful transitions.

Each person's *body budget* is shaped by a range of factors; for early educators this means the amount of energy, patience and emotional capacity we have to draw on can fluctuate from day to day. In busy Early Years environments, our own budgets can become depleted through constant demands, sensory load and emotional labour. When a child is perceived as misbehaving, it can be helpful to reframe this as a moment where someone's body budget is out of balance, whether that is the child's, the adult's, or both. Responding with punishment or harsh discipline often leads to further withdrawals, increasing stress for everyone involved. A more supportive question for us to hold is: in this moment, are our expectations creating more withdrawals than deposits, and what small adjustments might help rebalance both the child's budget and our own?

Activity 3.2 Thinking about body budgets

As a team, think about your body budgets and the withdrawals and deposits that are needed for you to have a good day. The likelihood is if we are off balance, our children will also be off balance. Time spent reflecting on our own needs eventually benefits the child.

Withdrawals might look like:

- being in ratio in the morning without a break or chance to take five minutes out of the room;
- morning handovers with parents and the transitions of children into the setting.

(Continued)

Deposits might look like:

- children playing outside and getting messy (much less contained);
- getting to sit on your lunchbreak in the cosy staff room uninterrupted with a big cup of coffee.

Conclusion

The role of the early educator is an incredible privilege. The work we do, though so often undervalued, is of huge importance in laying strong foundations, scaffolds and springboards for the future. What we offer in the Early Years does, in many ways, equip children with resources they will draw on for the rest of their lives. We do not say this in a deterministic way, or to place unnecessary pressure on you. We say it because it is a significant opportunity to offer children a wide repertoire of skills, knowledge and embodied experiences that they can draw on as life throws at them the highs, the lows, the flows and the in-betweens.

Not every experience will be positive. Life is unpredictable and learning how to move within that unpredictability is part of what readiness really is. But we cannot support this effectively if we do not take time to explore our own self-regulation capacity, including our wellbeing and our welldoing. As we wrote this chapter, it mattered to us that early educators know that they matter. So often you are undermined, overlooked, underpaid and, yes, looked down upon. And yet the role itself is deeply skilled and specialist. To care for and educate children under five takes a particular kind of person. Putting yourself in the strongest possible position, mentally and physically, means you are then able to truly offer the best of yourself as a role model for the children in your care. We know that, as early educators, you are likely already time-deprived. Drawing on so many of your own emotional, social and physical resources when you encounter the complexity of behaviours, it can help to have a framework by which to organise your thinking. This brings us to the *building blocks approach* also known as BEES.

References

Aldred, K.L. and Aldred, D. (2023) *Embodied Education: Creating Safe Space for Learning, Facilitating and Sharing*. Self-published.

Barrett, L.F. (2020) Your brain is not for thinking. *The New York Times*, 23 November.

Chen, F., Ge, Y., Xu, W., Yu, J., Zhang, Y., Xu, X. and Zhang, S. (2023) Changing kindergarten teachers' mindsets toward children to overcome compassion fatigue. *Psychology Research and Behavior Management*, 16, 521–33. https://doi.org/10.2147/PRBM.S396467

Frivold Kostøl, E.M. and Cameron, D.L. (2020) Teachers' responses to children in emotional distress: a study of co-regulation in the first year of primary school in Norway. *Education 3–13*, 49(7), 821–31.

Hochschild, A.R. (1983) *The Managed Heart: Commercialization of Human Feeling*. University of California Press.

Kesäläinen, J., Suhonen, E., Saha, M. and Sajaniemi, N. (2022) Children's stress activation in integrated early childhood special education and its connections to special educational needs and temperament. *European Early Childhood Education Research Journal*, 30(3), 456–71.

Max Planck Institute for Human Cognitive and Brain Sciences (2014) Your stress is my stress: observing stress can trigger a physical stress response. *Science Daily*, 3 May.

Moxley, K. (n.d.) *Early Years Consultancy and Training with Wellness for All*. https://wellnessforall.org.uk/early_years/

Murray, G.C. (2022) *Illuminating Care: The Pedagogy and Practice of Care in Early Childhood Communities*. Exchange Press.

Nicholson, J., Perez, L. and Kurtz, J. (2018) *Trauma-informed Practices for Early Childhood Educators: Relationship-based Approaches that Support Healing and Build Resilience in Young Children*. Routledge.

Ollison, J. (2019) Improving teacher retention by addressing teachers' compassion fatigue. Doctoral dissertation, University of the Pacific.

Stein, R., Garay, M. and Nguyen, A. (2022) It matters: early childhood mental health, educator stress, and burnout. *Early Childhood Education Journal*, 52, 333–44. https://doi.org/10.1007/s10643-022-01438-8

Zaki, J. (2019) *The War for Kindness: Building Empathy in a Fractured World*. Crown.

Zwolak, S. (2018) *What Happens Early in Life and the Importance of Early Childhood Education* [TEDx talk]. 22 May. www.ted.com/talks/steve_zwolak_what_happens_early_in_life_importance_of_early_childhood_education

4
Regulating landscapes
What this environment communicates about behaviour

When plants begin to wilt and wither away, we immediately provide the environment they need. We don't lecture, threaten or argue with their conditions.

Lori L. Desautels (2020)

Provocation: Are you jumping in or being pushed?

Imagine a swimming pool. Some children jump right into the pool with confidence, curiosity and trust. They approach the edge, dip a toe in and choose when and how they enter.

Other children venture cautiously to the ledge, reluctant and scared. To them, the pool does not feel welcoming. It is not an environment they would choose to enter.

In this scenario, however, all children must enter the pool. Whereas some jump in, others are pushed.

An environment compatible with children's needs

Several months ago, I watched an online webinar hosted by autistic charity Yellow Ladybugs. Two speakers (Robertson and Britton, 2025) spoke of an analogy that was useful when thinking about environments.

When you think about children coming into your environment, imagine it as a swimming pool. Some children are happy to enter and choose to jump in. These are the moments when the environment feels safe, predictable and aligned with their sensory, emotional and relational needs. The child is jumping in because the conditions support them to do so.

For other children, the experience is different. Although they might still come into the environment, it might feel to these children that they are being pushed. They are still in the same pool, but their sense of agency has been replaced with urgency. Their behaviours might look like resistance, hesitation, withdrawal, dysregulation or distress.

These are not signs of incapacity. They are signs that the environment is not yet compatible with the child's needs.

This chapter invites you to reflect on the environments you create and the experiences within them. Are children choosing to jump in because they feel supported, understood and welcomed? Or are they being pushed in by routines, sensory demands, social expectations or adult-led agendas that do not yet match their rhythms?

Introduction

We were recently reading *Take Action on Distraction* by Wass and Goldenberg (2025) and one idea stayed with us: the notion that the environment is often competing for children's attention. The authors describe how the layout, aesthetics, features and overall feel of a space can either support teaching and caregiving or undermine it. For example, you may be sat reading a story to a group of children and notice that they are very restless and distracted. It might be that they are expected to sit upright and still for the story, or that behind the educator is lots of visual noise that draw in the children's attention. Reading this through a behavioural lens prompted us to reflect on the many times we have told children off for not paying attention, appearing distracted, or moving restlessly around a space, without fully recognising the role the environment itself plays in shaping mood, action and behaviour.

The environment is constantly communicating with children and children often will respond to it. It sends messages through light, noise, layout, movement and visual detail, offering both spoken and unspoken cues about how to behave. This led us to reflect not only on our own practice, but also on our current roles supporting early childhood settings and schools. We have also come to realise that talking about the impact of the environment on engagement, learning, development and behaviour can be surprisingly difficult. I was reminded of this while delivering training during an INSET, when I gently suggested that aspects of the environment might feel overwhelming or restrictive for some children. I could see the lead educator become immediately defensive and protective of the space. I understood why especially as I was only seeing a snapshot of that space rather than the day to day running. Also, for most early educators, decisions about the environment are made with care, intention and the best interests of children in mind. To hear that the space might be hindering children's experiences can feel personal and uncomfortable.

In that moment, I held in mind what else I knew about this leader. They had shared countless examples of their advocacy for children and demonstrated deep reflection in many areas of their practice. They were confident that the environment worked. I chose not to push further. Yet this moment stayed with me because adapting and evolving our environments requires a willingness to acknowledge that early childhood spaces can sometimes be one of the biggest triggers for behaviour.

In this chapter, we have resisted jumping into how to set up your environment for pro-social behaviours because we think the environment is so much more than a set up. What we want to emphasise in this chapter is some of the spoken and unspoken routines, rhythms and rules that are communicated. That is to say, we walk into many beautiful, inspiring, well-resourced spaces, but the emotional climate and behavioural practices can feel unwelcoming to children. These spoken and unspoken elements are often designed to manage behaviour, but they can unintentionally restrict learning and development or even escalate the very behaviours we are trying to reduce. If environments can escalate behaviour, they can also steady it. The same space that overwhelms can be reshaped to regulate, communicate safety and reduce the need for behavioural correction. We will do this by exploring our regulating landscapes.

Regulating landscapes

Imagine a child walking into an Early Years environment that has lots of space and is open. The instinct of this child might be to run or move freely because the landscape itself appears to welcome this. But then an educator points to some posters on the wall that suggest children should have 'walking feet', 'quiet voices' and 'kind hands'. This can be really confusing and contradictory to a child who can see a landscape that communicates or invites something different. Children behave and regulate in response to the landscapes *they see*. Before any adult instruction, the environment is already communicating what bodies and minds are allowed, expected or discouraged to do. For example:

- an open, uncluttered space invites speed, movement and expansion;
- a narrow or enclosed space invites containment;
- soft materials such as cushions and blankets might invite rest or quality time;
- repetitive resources invite flow.

Children will often respond to these environmental cues instinctively, not deliberately based on their prior experiences. When a child runs in an open space, they are responding to the capacity of that space. They are responding logically to what the environment affords. If that same space communicates 'walking feet' through adult rules rather than environmental design, the landscape becomes confusing for a child who may not be able to understand the adult's logic.

Regulating landscapes ask us to look and consider:

- what does this space invite a body and mind to do?
- what kind of energy does this environment afford or suppress?
- are we asking children to override bodily cues rather than designing spaces that support them?

When environments are intentionally designed with this in mind they can do some of the regulation work for us. As educators, we have such a high-intensity role when it comes to supporting behaviour that we want the environment to help us rather than hinder us. A developmentally informed environment reduces the need for constant correction and increases children's capacity to co-regulate, collectively regulate and self-regulate through the environment itself. Regulation is no longer something children are told to do, but something they are experiencing and making sense of. Thinking in terms of regulating landscapes encourages us to reflect on what our environments communicate to children about how to behave, and where those messages may be unclear, restrictive or missing altogether.

Regulation as meaning, not mood: Does the space enable sense-making and meaning-making?

One of the points myself and Sarah have made throughout the book is that regulation and developing pro-social behaviours are ongoing learning experiences happening across different contexts. Our early childhood settings offer a space in which we can build capacity for regulation by enabling access. However, too often spaces become places of compliance where access to regulation can be suppressed. When regulation is viewed solely through calm states or engaging in ways that are deemed acceptable by adults, children begin to perform regulation as per these expectations. When we think about children's developmental experiences of regulation, we want to ensure that children have opportunities to find meaning in the way they regulate. This will support them to feel better equipped for the things that life might throw at them (both the good and the bad stuff). There are many ways in which we might help children to make meaning – for example, through representative emotional literacy where children can have *mirrors, windows* and *sliding glass doors* into emotional worlds (Bishop, 1990).

- Mirrors – I can make sense of myself here.
- Windows – I can make sense of others here.
- Doors – I can step into experiences that are not my own.

(Bishop, 1990)

Expectations and invisible rules: What behaviour fits naturally here and what behaviour is corrected?

We always find it strange that the rules of an environment are often decided way before we meet a child or group of children. We set up our spaces and we, the grown-ups, decide how that space is going to work. I have written about this in countless other books and made the point that the early education space or classroom is often viewed as belonging to the adult, with the child coming into our space, even though technically it is their space. Given that there is so much out there about the importance of children being collaborators in their own learning, and how important it is to have their own voice, there is often very little happening in terms of how children shape the social 'rules' and expectations. They are usually told what is happening and they are expected to follow this even if some of those expectations don't necessarily make sense.

Environments usually have the rules plastered up on the walls with behavioural expectations, and there can be a tendency to believe that children should not question the rules. This 'because I said so' mentality is something we both heard a lot as children, and it is something we have both also said in our early childhood spaces. There are many reasons why we might say this – for example:

- … because we are the adults and we know better;
- or we are just goddam tired in the midst of a ten-hour day and children love to ask the same questions over and over, repeat the same disgruntles or just generally have the attitude of 'Why though?'
- because them's the rules (even if the rules make no sense).

We are not saying your environment should not have guidelines and agreements, but we have found that they should be collaborative and developed with children. I discovered a long ago-delivered training session where I had worked with a setting who introduced 'agreements' with the children; their *golden rules* were decided in community with the children. Here are some examples, with affirmations.

- We wriggle because it helps us to listen (Child, 4).
- I share if I want to, I don't if I don't want to (Child, 5).
- Being calm feels nice, and my friends help me to be nice (Child, 4).
- Sitting down hurts my bum so I'll try to listen until my bum hurts (Child, 3).
- I do the pufferfish when I want to talk (Child, 4).
- If I am sad, I will have snuggles (Child, 3).
- I like being nice to my friends because they are my favourite (Child, 4).

Sometimes, the 'because I said so' mentality can be triggering for children who need to know the logic of a rule or expectation. We talk about this through reason to regulate.

Reason to regulate

Reason to regulate is what is says on the tin … it is having practices within your environment that take time to ensure children can make sense of the rules, routines and rhythms and expectations.

Put it into practice: Explainer expectations

For some children, it helps to know why an expectation is place – for example, 'We need to walk in this space, so we don't bump into each other.'

Why before what

Before providing an instruction, provide the why so the reasoning is clear – for example, 'So we have space to sit comfortably, you might want to draw a big circle around yourself, so you have space to move without touching others.'

See it to do it …

Visuals, such as sequences that show expectations, can help children to make sense of those expectations – for example, a photo schedule of where to place belongings when coming indoors.

Ditch nonsensical rules

Sometimes children will call out things that do not make sense. They question things – not because they are being defiant, but because they are looking for the sense. If we say, 'quiet hands' to a child who loves to express using their hands, and they question this … we need to also question why we have 'said so'.

Case study: Shouting out

I was working with an Early Years setting that was focused on school readiness. They shared with me that one of the expectations of children once they go to school is to raise their hands before answering. Children were asked to raise their hands when taking part in circle time. I noticed that when this was happening, children would often get excited to give an answer and contribute. Sometimes their engagement led to impulsive answers rather than remembering to put hands up. Children would be reminded of the rules and on occasion, told off for not waiting. While we do need to have ways to ensure children can take turns answering, I picked up that children were being told off for not putting their hands up and their contributions were dismissed, even when they gave the right answer. We talked afterwards about the ways in which this practice could be quite disheartening for a child who had engaged and answered but the focus was more on behaviour than being involved in the activity. We then discussed ways in which we could increase impulse control instead of focusing solely on hands up (see Put it into practice below).

Put it into practice: Moving beyond 'hands up'

- Invite *collective answering* (for example, 'Ready ... steady ... go') to support shared engagement, anticipation, patience and collaboration rather than individual competition.
- Use *impulsive engagement intentionally*, recognising that children often want to respond immediately and that this can be channelled rather than suppressed.
- Vary how children respond using a *question-and-answer dial*, such as whispering answers, shouting together, saying responses slowly or quickly, or passing answers along. This builds cognitive flexibility and reduces reliance on one 'right' way to participate.
- Offer *non-verbal and written response routes*, such as posting answers, questions, thoughts, or feelings into a classroom post-box. This supports children who find spoken responses demanding or anxiety-provoking.
- Use *talking tools or props* instead of static hand-raising, making turn-taking visible, playful and supportive for children who feel cautious about speaking.
- Prioritise *actions over spoken answers* by inviting children to show, find, copy, choose, or move rather than respond verbally. This reduces pressure and supports multimodal participation.
- Replace frequent direct questioning with *declarative language* (for example, 'I wonder ...') and shared thinking structures to reduce cognitive load and disengagement.
- Notice that expanding participation beyond 'hands up' supports *regulation, confidence and critical thinking*, not just behaviour compliance.

Emotional permission: Which feelings are allowed to exist here?

There can sometimes be a tendency for educators to assume that *emotional permission* means allowing children to express emotions and behaviours that may be harmful, without boundaries or response. This is not what emotional permission entails. Throughout this book, we have explored emotional agency in early childhood, recognising that children gradually develop awareness of their emotions and energy states, how these are experienced internally and how they impact others.

Early educators play a crucial role in supporting this process through emotion work that helps children make sense of themselves and their relationships. However, this work carries a risk. When emotions and behaviours are addressed without care, children may internalise shame about who they are, rather than developing responsibility for what they have done. Helen Block Lewis (1913–1987) highlighted this distinction, differentiating shame ('I am bad') from guilt ('I did

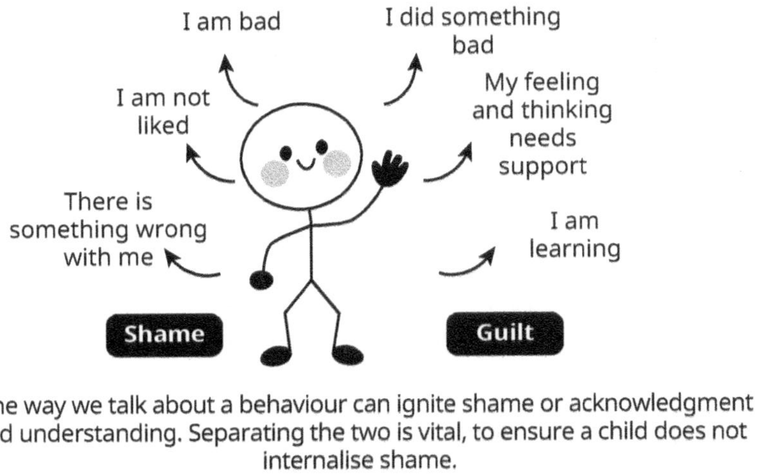

Figure 4.1 The difference between guilt and shame

something bad'). Holding this distinction allows educators to support children to develop awareness and agency, while understanding what they may or may not need to take responsibility for.

I recently observed an educator navigate this with particular skill. A conflict between two children arose and quickly dispersed. While the educator chose not to intervene in the moment, she recognised that some of the language used needed to be revisited. Addressing it at the height of emotion may have intensified distress or evoked shame. Instead, later on, she gently opened the conversation by asking, 'What was happening for you earlier when you were talking to Shannon?'

This approach created space to reflect on the interaction without blame. The educator acknowledged the child's feelings and then supported her to consider the impact of her words. She said, 'I can see why that made you feel angry. I noticed that when you are angry, you sometimes use names to show how you feel. I wonder how that felt for you, and how it might have felt for them?'

This interaction reflected the child's unique co-regulation blueprint, where talking things through was supportive. The educator chose her words carefully, not to induce shame, but to highlight the child's agency in recognising the impact of her behaviour and to support her in finding alternative ways to express difficult emotions.

Behaviour blueprints (old to new way of thinking)

Old blueprint: Behaviour as something to stop

'Biting is unacceptable.'

This stance reflects a binary view of behaviour where actions are quickly categorised as good or bad, acceptable or unacceptable. When we adopt this lens, our attention is pulled towards stopping the behaviour rather than understanding it.

The behaviour becomes the problem and the child's experience becomes secondary. This can lead to reactive responses, shame-based messages or missed opportunities to explore what the behaviour is communicating or protecting.

New blueprint: Behaviour as something to understand and resolve

'If I can find the function or reason for biting, I am more able to support finding a resolve.'

This stance shifts the focus away from moral judgement and towards curiosity, connection and developmental understanding. Instead of treating the behaviour as something to eliminate, we see it as a clue that points to an unmet need, sensory experience, stressor or developmental stage. When we understand the purpose behind the behaviour, we can respond more thoughtfully, adapt the environment, support co-regulation and teach skills that will serve the child over time.

Predictability as safety: Is the environment logical and meaningful?

Part of both of our roles involves moving through lots of unfamiliar environments, alongside those that have become familiar over time. Recently, I was visiting a setting and relied on the map on my phone to get me there. When I arrived at the pinned location, I could not see an entrance to the nursery. I walked around for almost ten minutes thinking, 'Why is there no signposting for this place?' Eventually, I found my way inside.

When I reached the reception desk and said hello, the receptionist kept her head down, focused on her work. I noticed a sign-in computer and logically assumed that was what I should do, so I signed in and returned to the desk to wait. The receptionist continued to ignore me. It was clear she was not particularly receptive to dealing with me. Eventually, I said, 'I am here to see …' and she reluctantly went to find the person I was visiting. The moment that person came to collect me, I felt an immediate sense of relief. I could finally relax as they guided me to where we would be meeting.

This is not simply a complaint about poor signposting or an unwelcoming receptionist. These things happen. What I am pointing to is something we often overlook. A world without predictability can be confusing. For me, as an autistic person who struggles to tolerate uncertainty, it is deeply dysregulating. That short experience left me feeling stressed, irritated and on edge.

As humans, we often assume that others know how an environment works or how they are expected to behave within it. In reality, many of us rely on cues, signals and shared understandings to help us navigate spaces safely and confidently. You might be thinking, 'But didn't you just say rules are problematic?' Yes, rules can be problematic. But this is not about rules. It is about clear cues and meaningful guidance that help people understand how to enter, move through and belong in a space. Predictability is not about control. It is about safety.

Table 4.1 Feature of predictability in practice

Feature of predictability	Description
Arrival and exits that makes sense to children	• Children know what happens when they arrive • There is a clear, consistent routine that helps them transition from home to setting • This might include a familiar greeting, a visual cue, or a predictable first activity. Children are not left wondering where to go or what to do next • Children are given time to acclimatise
Spaces that communicate their purpose	• The environment explains itself • Children can tell where they can move, play, rest, or retreat without needing constant adult direction • The layout, resources and boundaries of spaces give clear cues about how they can be used, while still allowing for creativity and divergence
Visuals are visible	• There is a consistent visual routine used • Visuals do not get lost in the visual noise of the setting • Multimodal visuals are used such as objects of reference, line drawings and photographs • Visuals are used in dynamic ways – for example, labelling and sequencing, and activity and routine mapping
Attuned educators	• Educators can tune into energy states, regulation rhythms and moods of children individually and collectively • Adults respond in ways children recognise • While adults adapt to individual needs, their tone, expectations and emotional availability are consistent • This consistency helps children anticipate adult responses and supports co-regulation rather than vigilance • Educators have their own routines and rhythms when they have lower bandwidth
Routines that create rhythm, not rigidity	• Predictable environments have a rhythm to the day: children know the general flow of what happens and when, even if the exact details vary • This rhythm supports regulation by reducing surprise and helping children prepare for transitions
Agreements made visible	• Children are not expected to infer social rules • Expectations are shown through modelling, visuals, shared language and gentle reminders • This supports children who do not naturally pick up implicit social cues and reduces shame-based corrections
Transitions that are scaffolded	• Predictability is strongest at moments of change. Children are supported with warnings, visuals, songs, or familiar prompts that help them anticipate what is coming next • The environmental features are used to support awareness and understanding of transitions such as dimming the lights for tidy-up time • Transitions are treated as moments requiring support, not compliance

Feature of predictability	Description
Sensory experiences that are coherent	• A predictable environment considers sensory load. Lighting, sound, textures, and visual information are intentionally balanced so that children are not constantly managing unexpected sensory input • Sensory predictability supports emotional regulation and engagement
Flexibility explained, not imposed	• When things change, children are supported to understand the change • Adults name what is different and what will stay the same • This helps children maintain a sense of safety even when routines shift
The space is dynamic but consistent	• The design of the space is not just to accommodate play and learning, but also rest, relaxation, movement, energetic states
A felt sense of being expected and welcomed	• Most importantly, the environment communicates to children, 'You belong here' • Their ways of moving, playing, communicating and regulating are anticipated and accommodated rather than corrected

Enabling embodiment: Can children exist fully in their minds and bodies here?

In the Early Years, we delight in children's movement. We celebrate crawling, rolling, climbing, reaching, wheeling, rocking, spinning, splashing and exploring the world through the full expression of their bodies. These moments are often met with joy in infancy and toddlerhood. Yet somewhere between the nursery and the schooling classroom, our openness to movement shifts. Instead of encouraging movement, we begin to control, shape and dictate it. Instead of recognising the body as a site of learning, sensory regulation and communication, we begin to treat it as something that must be subdued, sedentary and malleable.

Children enter education systems that are profoundly preoccupied with stillness. Children are told to sit still, calm down, stop fidgeting, use their walking feet and even to 'lock your mouths'. Just last year I sat during a lesson observation in a school where children were told to lock their mouths dozens of times within the space of 40 minutes. These everyday directives teach a powerful lesson: that their bodies do not belong to them, that comfort comes at the cost of compliance and that autonomy is conditional. The contradiction that Sarah and I have sat with is: why do we encourage so much bodily autonomy to only then take it away?

From a developmental perspective, this makes little sense. Movement is not a barrier to learning, rather it *is* the learning. Sure, it is sometimes messy, chaotic and difficult to handle, but the ways in which you gain capacity of your body is to be able to fully move in your body in safe ways. We always draw on the work of Connell and McCarthy, who teach us that a moving child is a learning child (2013), and the work of Ken Robinson (2015), who reminds us that children need to move to be able to think. Not only is the notion that children should learn to sit still by sitting still untrue, but it also imposes demands that are incompatible with how many children's nervous systems function. These expectations create environments in which dysregulation is interpreted as defiance, sensory needs are misread as misbehaviour and differences in embodiment become grounds for discipline.

Whole-body compliance, then, is not developmentally meaningful. It asks children to suppress instinctive regulation in order to perform school readiness. It disproportionately harms neurodivergent and disabled children, for whom movement, stimming, positional changes and bodily expression are vital ways of staying connected, grounded and safe.

What children need is not compliance but connection. They need adults who understand that movement is communication, stimming is a valid form of engagement and that bodies have knowledge of their own. Shifting from whole-body compliance to whole-body affirmation is a pedagogical change, but it is also a cultural one. It signals to children that their comfort matters, that their bodies are trustworthy and that learning does not require performance of stillness. It invites curricula that honour joy, playfulness, sensory movement and the natural rhythms of human energy. It asks educators to practise bodily empathy, recognising that children's bodies are their own and shared regulation is essential to an environment that creates harmony.

Figure 4.2 Example of whole-body listening versus whole-body affirmations

Case study: Movement for me but not for you

I was recently working with a trainee teacher in a reception class. While I was observing her practice, I noticed that she was quite flustered at children moving or fidgeting during her teaching input. She became so distracted by it that the lesson did not get completed. I sat and thought about how I might address this without making the teacher feel defensive or disheartened. Weirdly, I noted in the observation that she was quite expressive in her teaching style, often using her hands to gesture and demonstrate, and she also moved a lot herself. After the lesson, I asked her how she might feel if I gave feedback to her to suggest that when she was teaching, she should stay as still as possible and not fidget. She said that this would interfere with her teaching quality as movement helps her to express herself and to get her thoughts out into words. I followed this up with 'If you can afford this understanding for yourself, why can you not afford this understanding for the children who wanted to move to engage during your lesson?' This simple comparison gave enough food for thought for this teacher in that moment. When we spoke a few months later, she shared how she had begun to incorporate movement for the children into her teaching and began modelling how movement helped her to think.

Case study: Resistance isn't futile

I am a key person in a busy day nursery. One of the ways in which children exercise their sense of belonging is often through acts of resistance. That might seem counterintuitive, but I've learned that the testing of boundaries is sometimes a child exploring how accepted they are. For example, a child continually refused to sit down with others during snack time. He would simply deny the request to sit with his peers. When we spoke to his parents, they explained that breakfast was an important part of their morning routine and their child often loved a 'big breakfast'. By the time he got to nursery, he found an additional snack too much. His resistance wasn't misbehaviour, rather it was a reflection that the situation wasn't in tune with his daily routine. He was being taken away from play to meet the 'rules' of a routine that simply didn't need to be there. We agreed that morning snack shouldn't be so rigid and, actually, a rolling snack might be more flexible. We didn't want the child to develop negative associations with the meal area; in fact, this change in response to his resistance was for the good of us all. Belonging is about reading those cues of resistance as a child finding how the environment fits in with their world view.

To better understand the concept of attunement, Braman (2021) suggests we think of it as being 'in tune' with another person. When we form relationships with the children we care for there will be moments where we need to focus our attention on them to ensure they feel heard, understood and supported. It's important to note that attunement doesn't necessarily mean fulfilling every need, but rather recognising the existence of a need. Through attunement, we gain deeper insights into the child and become aware of their unique set of needs. Braman highlights that, with time, attunement also involves the ability to anticipate someone's needs and emotions. We begin to interpret the child's cues and understand cues like 'they are hungry' or 'their face turning red often leads to a meltdown'. Being attuned to another person may feel like a significant responsibility, but for children who may seem more challenging to understand, we may need to focus our attention on them even more to develop attunement.

Put it into practice: Scan for satisfiers and disatisfiers

'I have noticed that when it is really loud in here, you can get overwhelmed. Let me know next time if it's too loud. We have the volume button.'

Be environmentally aware ...

Max-Neef (1991) used the term 'satisfiers' to emphasise actions, spaces, structures and processes that contribute to the fulfilment of needs, while 'dissatisfiers' hinder or fail to meet the needs. I often use this to scan the environment and look for satisfiers or dissatisfiers. For example:

- the children as a group appear to be experiencing high energy and stress – the bright lights and all windows closed are a dissatisifer, so I will dim the light and open a few windows to enable the environment;
- children know that there are cosy spaces to go and hide during the day – this becomes a satisfier for their needs;
- lots of children like to join in with the sensory tabletop activity, but the chairs have become a dissastifier as they limit movement and the number of children who can join. Removing the chairs enables children to stand around.

Are behaviour charts still a thing?

I was recently delivering some training to a group of early educators and I referred to the use of behaviour charts. One of the participants turned to me and said, 'Those were around when I started out 30 years ago, surely, they are not still a thing.' I found this quite interesting as, in all the schools and settings I visit, I would say most schools have a public behaviour chart system still. They are used via rewards and sanctions systems and often positioned as a way of creating a safe classroom community.

Now, children do need to learn how to live alongside others. Understanding shared expectations helps children feel orientated, safe and able to participate in community life. However, systems that rely on public shaming are never an appropriate way to support this learning. Their use reflects a deeper issue: the dehumanisation of children. Behaviour charts, traffic light systems and public displays of 'good' and 'bad' behaviour are often defended as neutral or motivating tools. They operate by exposing children's perceived failures to others. They rely on embarrassment, fear of negative attention or social comparison to suppress behaviour. This may appear to work in the short term, but the emotional and developmental cost is significant.

Public shaming as harm, not pedagogy

The harm caused by public shaming is not hypothetical. In 2019, the *Guardian* reported on the case of a ten-year-old autistic child whose behaviour was described by his school as disruptive and difficult to manage (Jayanetti, 2019). As a corrective exercise, he was asked to draw a picture of himself and share it with his peers. The class was then invited to write down his 'annoying' traits on the picture, framed by the question, 'How can I get the other children to like me?' This activity was explicitly used to eliminate these traits. This example is extreme, but it reveals the logic underpinning many shaming systems. The child is positioned as the problem. Their identity becomes the target of intervention, rather than the environment, the expectations or the unmet needs driving the behaviour. For neurodivergent children in particular, public shaming intersects with trauma and bullying. Repeated exposure to these systems reinforces feelings of shame, difference and social exclusion, often long after the behaviour itself has passed.

'But my chart isn't used like that'

Across many years of working with educators, a familiar pattern of defence emerges. Educators often argue that their behaviour charts are not used in extreme ways, that most systems work well, or that children simply need to learn who is in charge. These arguments rest on the assumption that if a system appears to function, it must be harmless. Within education 'we have always done it this way' is often used as a justification for continuing to engage in practices that might feel harmful to others.

This assumption also ignores the wider cultural impact of systems that normalise shame as a tool for control. Even when used 'gently', public behaviour systems create a hierarchy of worth, where some children are consistently visible as successful and others are repeatedly exposed as failing. Over time, this becomes a systems culture, not an isolated strategy.

The cost to self-regulation and identity

Behaviour charts are often mistakenly framed as tools for self-regulation. In reality, they diminish it. Punishment-based systems work by increasing stress, not by developing new skills. For some children, negative attention is familiar or unavoidable. Over time, their identity becomes fixed as 'the bad child'. A telling feature of these systems is their lack of impact. The child who is 'on red' today is frequently the same child who was 'on red' yesterday, and the day before, and likely will be again tomorrow. When an intervention does not lead to meaningful change, it is not the child who has failed. It is the strategy.

What do we aim for instead?

If compliance is not the goal, then what is? Alternatives to shaming centre habits and dispositions that support long-term learning and wellbeing. These include autonomy, self-advocacy, self-regulation, engagement, intrinsic motivation and joy. These are not cultivated through fear or exposure, but through relationship, understanding and meaningful support. Children thrive when feedback acts as a hook for engagement rather than a running commentary on failure. Constant correction erodes confidence and motivation, leading to withdrawal or behaviour as a means of escape. Individual affirmations, grounded in genuine recognition of strengths, offer children stepping stones towards success without attaching worth to compliance.

Creating stepping stones rather than sanctions

Rather than imposing rules onto children, educators can collaborate with individuals and groups to identify helpful habits. When children understand that expectations exist to support safety, participation and connection, they are far more likely to engage with them. This includes explaining expectations clearly and respectfully. Children are capable of empathy and understanding when adults model it. Simple, honest explanations of how behaviour affects others often elicit cooperation far more effectively than commands or consequences.

Misbehaviour or dysregulation?

Moving away from shame-based systems is not quick or easy. These approaches are deeply embedded in educational culture and are often defended through habit, fear or perceived control. Ditching them requires time, reflection and courage. If a system does not feel right, it probably is not right, for the child or for the adult. Ethical practice in behaviour support demands that we are willing to question tools that prioritise control over dignity, even when they are familiar or widely accepted.

Activity 4.1 Evaluating space and behaviours

Grab a large piece of paper and create a bird's-eye view of one early childhood space in your setting. You may wish to sketch key features or indicators – for example, a square to represent the water tray. Draw lines to map out different zones, such as the snack area or reading corner.

Within each zone, discuss:

- what behaviour do we expect in this space?
- based on how the space is designed, what behaviour does it actually invite?
- how do neighbouring zones influence or spill into this space?

Next, use a colour-coding system to reflect how regulation is currently supported.

- *Green*: where regulation seems supported by the environment itself (for example, soft furnishings inviting rest, or clear boundaries inviting containment).
- *Amber*: where children regularly need reminders, corrections or prompts.
- *Red*: where children are frequently corrected, shamed, or asked to comply against their instincts.

Encourage noticing patterns across the space rather than focusing on individual children.
Ask:

- where are we asking children to behave against what the space invites?
- where are we relying on rules instead of design?

Rather than redesigning everything, choose one micro-change to trial, such as:

- changing the layout rather than changing the language used with children;
- adding a visual cue instead of repeating a verbal rule;
- creating a movement route rather than suppressing movement;
- making expectations visible rather than inferred.

The emphasis is on designing for regulation, not managing behaviour.

If you need further prompting, consider the examples below.

Expanding a high-interest space

'We noticed that the sand and water area was extremely popular and many children wanted to access it at the same time. We placed a cap on numbers, but conflicts were frequent. We eventually realised that sand and water play was such a strong motivator that scarcity was the issue. We expanded the area and made a lesser-used space slightly smaller. We also introduced a choice board so children could access water and sand play in different ways, such as indoors, outdoors, standing or at a table. This reduced competition and helped children feel less restricted.'

Designing for movement

'Children in this space loved moving between areas, but we were constantly giving safety and behaviour reminders. Chairs were left pulled out, children tripped over them and conflicts arose when seats were taken. We realised the space prioritised sitting, even though we wanted children to move freely. We introduced more free-standing desks and reduced the number of chairs. For exploratory play this has been really beneficial, as children no longer feel contained at a table.'

Routines that make sense

'Tidy-up time took a long time, and children often threw resources into boxes without care. At the end of the day, we had to reorganise everything, which felt frustrating. On reflection, we realised there was no clear 'home' for resources and no visual cues to support children. We introduced a clearer visual system that matched boxes to shelves, helping children understand where things belong and supporting more purposeful tidying.'

Intersectionality insight: No such thing as normal

I recently published a book, *Neurodiversity-affirming Practices in Early Childhood* (Murphy, 2025), where I wrote about the concept of neuronormativity in the early childhood space. Neuronormativity can be defined as *the belief that there is a correct, right, or superior way to function as a human* (Wise, 2023). It is based on a relatively narrow set of social norms, expectations and behaviours that humans must meet to be seen as 'normal' (a social construct). This shapes how we are allowed to think, feel, process, sense, play, learn, pay attention, regulate, behave and interact. Humans are often categorised according to their capacity to conform or not – for example, normal vs abnormal, neurotypical vs neurodivergent, typical vs special, which segregates children into experiences of privilege or marginalisation (Murphy, 2025; Wise, 2023).

When we think about children's behaviours, it is important to recognise that we sometimes may make judgements on a child's behaviour based on what we expect to see. In other words, what is typical or 'normal'. But normal is a social construction and one which often leads to some children's behaviours being considered acceptable and others not acceptable. In the early education space, it is not uncommon for neurodivergent and disabled children's behaviours to be deemed as not fitting the norm; this might also be viewed through a deficit lens. For example, a child may engage in self-stimulatory and repetitive behaviours, also known as stimming. For this, they may be told to have 'quiet hands' or to stop fidgeting. You may even find that they are put in interventions that train them out of this stimming behaviour. And yet, we increasingly know that stimming can have supportive functions as a way of regulating, communicating, playing and expressing oneself. When we think about our social rules, norms and codes of behaviour, we have to also think about whether they can intentionally or unintentionally exclude behaviours that are traits of neurodivergence or disability.

Conclusion

The environment can act as a powerful regulator, not only for the child, but for you as the educator too. Yet, too often, the environment can end up undermining us or competing against us. Children and adults spend many hours together in early childhood spaces and intentional, sensitive and informed design can support success rather than become a risk to it. Across this chapter, we have explored just some of the ways you can develop an evolving and responsive environment.

As we have stated throughout, the environment ultimately belongs to the child, so it must reflect their lived experiences, differences and needs. We have also considered the spoken and unspoken norms communicated through our environments, alongside the daily routines and rhythms that can sometimes create rigid expectations around behaviour, such as demands for stillness, compliance and rule-following.

No two environments will ever look the same, and there is no single model of what your environment should be. Rather, what matters is that you create predictable and secure foundations from which children can creatively shape the space over time.

And this brings us to our penultimate chapter. Early education is a space where learning and development are rightly valued. But there can also be such a strong emphasis on productivity and readiness agendas that children are not always given enough time to simply be. In the next chapter, we explore the importance of rest, flow and rise in honouring regulation and behaviour.

References

Bishop, R.S. (1990) Windows and mirrors: children's books and parallel cultures. *California State University Reading Conference: 14th Annual Conference Proceedings*. March (pp. 3–12).

Braman, L. (2021) *Understanding How Attunement and Containment Help Form Attachments*. 21 September. https://lindsaybraman.com/attunement-containment-attachment/?utm_source=chatgpt.com

Connell, G. and McCarthy, C. (2013) *A Moving Child is a Learning Child: How the Body Teaches the Brain to Think (Birth to Age 7)*. Free Spirit.

Desautels, L. L. (2020). *Connections over compliance: Rewiring our perceptions of discipline*. Wyatt-MacKenzie.

Jayanetti, C. (2019) Teachers 'forced special needs child to make a list of his faults'. *Guardian*, 28 July. www.theguardian.com/education/2019/jul/28/derby-primary-school-boy-with-special-needs-blamed-for-being-bullied

Lewis, H.B. (1971) Shame and guilt in neurosis. *Psychoanalytic Review*, 58(3), 419.

Max-Neef, M. (1991) *Human Scale Development: Conception, Application and Further Reflections*. Apex Press.

Murphy, K. (2025) *Neurodiversity-affirming Practices in Early Childhood: An Empowering Guide to Diverse Development and Play*. Routledge.

Robertson, S. and Britton, C. (2025) Supporting the sensory needs of our ladybugs [conference session]. *Yellow Ladybugs 2025 Conference*. www.yellowladybugs.com.au/About/Conference

Robinson, K. (2015) *Creative Schools: The Grassroots Revolution That's Transforming Education*. Penguin.

Wass, S. and Goldenberg, G. (2025) *Take Action on Distraction: The Definitive Guide to Improving Attention and Focus in the Early Years and Key Stage One*. Bloomsbury Education.

Wise, S.J. (2023) *We're All Neurodiverse: How to Build a Neurodiversity-affirming Future and Challenge Neuronormativity*. Jessica Kingsley.

5

Rest, flow and activate

The right to rest, flow and energy states

The child's mind and body is a site of liberation.

It does not belong to capitalism or endless productivity.

Let them love their mind and body.

Let them rest their mind and body.

Let them embody.

Let them hold the boundaries of their mind and body.

Adapted from Hersey, 2022

Provocation: The child's perspective

Imagine the early childhood environment from the child's perspective. You arrive in a world that once revolved almost entirely around your comfort, rhythms, needs and safety. Then, suddenly, you are immersed in a setting full of people, noise, movement, rules, expectations, sensory input and social complexity. For many children, this is exciting. There is play, exploration, discovery and connection. But it is also a lot. A lot for the brain. A lot for the body. A lot for the nervous system.

Creating environments that support different regulation and energy states: the flat and fizzy pop analogy

This is an analogy you might have heard before, but we return to it here because it beautifully sets the scene for this block in our framework.

One of the things we often talk to early educators and teachers about is the sheer intensity of early childhood environments. And here is where the pop comes in.

Sometimes children are like fizzy pop. Everything is bursting, bubbling and overflowing. There is too much input, too much demand, too much noise, too many transitions, too many expectations. The fizz rises and rises until it is no longer excitement, but agitation, overwhelm or distress. We often recognise this as dysregulation quickly because it is loud, visible and can be disruptive.

But sometimes children can experience the flat pop feeling because there is not enough stimulation and not enough engagement. The fizz has gone. And yet, this flatness too is also a state of stress. Understimulation can feel like fog, shutdown, restlessness, disconnection or quiet distress. It is easier to miss because the child appears calm and compliant.

Both flat and fizzy pop are forms of nervous system stress. One is too much. The other is not enough. And neither is where learning, wellbeing or belonging exist.

This is why this building block matters so deeply. Children do not just need to be 'calmed down'. They need opportunities to rest, space to flow and moments to experience high energy states. They need environments that can soften the fizz without flattening them and lift the flat without overwhelming them. It is about designing for that balance, about noticing when children are over-filled, when they are under-filled and how we intentionally shape environments, rhythms and relationships so children can move between rest, engagement and renewed energy in ways that feel safe and sustainable.

Introduction

Earlier on in the book we explored the problem of only seeing regulation as calm. In this chapter, we are going to expand beyond concepts of calm and introduce insights into the different energy states a child might experience across the day in recognition that as humans we fluctuate and transition through different energy states based on what we need in that moment to feel well and to do well. Regulation is so much more than being calm and calm itself is so much more than taking a few deep breaths or following an adult's instructions under the guise of co-regulation.

A few years ago, a friend introduced me to the Nap Ministry (Hershey, 2022) which was founded by Tricia Hersey in 2016. She describes it as an organisation that examines the liberating power of naps; it delivers this through a 'rest is resistance' framework that draws on different disciplines such as performance art and creating safe spaces to nap. I remember following along on the Instagram™ page and just feeling exhilaration at the promotion of napping, especially as someone that loves to nap. I genuinely believe life would be better for us all if there were designated spaces for napping for grown-ups. The Nap Ministry is not just about laziness, though laziness is a valid state; it is rooted in social justice work including anti-racism and anti-ableism. It recognises that we live in societies and cultures that over-emphasise constant productivity and input; this begins in early childhood through agendas such as school readiness and learning through play. We communicate early on to children that we need to *grow out* of rest, play, relaxation and flow states, and we replace this with diligence, compliance and grind culture. So, for

Hersey, rest is not simply a leisurely thing to do, but it actively resists the demands placed on the human mind and body. After I took a nap, I started to explore rest in relation to early education. Alongside Tricia Hersey's work, I also stumbled upon an amazing TED talk and article by Saundra Dalton-Smith (2019). It completely transformed how I understood regulation for both children and adults.

Working nine to five

Children in the Early Years are often taught and trained to deny themselves rest in preparation for schooling which can operate like a nine to five workday. You clock in, you are productive and you clock out. Another common metaphor used is referred to as the *factory system of schooling*. To talk about rest as resistance, we first need to understand where schooling came from. Early schools and access to education was not originally designed to control children or restrict them. Due to the industrial revolution, many were created with the hopeful intentions that they could improve lives, provide social mobility and produce more efficient labour. Early education reformers believed learning environments should support the whole child, with access to fresh air, natural light, movement, play and social connection. These were seen as essential for learning and wellbeing, not distractions from it.

The problem with modern education and increasingly unstable political landscapes is not that it has industrial roots, it is more that we have not evolved enough or moved with the times. We continue to deliver education drawing on the bleaker aspects of the factory. Over time, schooling has become increasingly focused on efficiency, routines, targets and measurable outcomes. This has led to environments that prioritise timetables, productivity and performance over children's wellbeing, relationships and natural rhythms. In many settings, rest is treated as something to earn, manage, or minimise rather than something children genuinely need.

Positioning rest as resistance means pushing back against this narrow focus, especially in early childhood where we increasingly experience top-down pressures. For example, fields such as developmentalism suggest that all children are developing through stages and successful progression through this prepares the child for learning (Burman, 2017). But human development is simply not this straightforward and stages of development are too often reinterpreted through predefined educational goals. When we prioritise outcome over experience and compliance over connection, we can lose sight of children's lived experiences. We are not just getting them ready for work, but for life. When we prioritise rest, we are not lowering expectations or reducing ambition. We are reclaiming an older and more human idea of education – one that recognises children as relational, social and embodied learners.

All work and no play

When we focus solely on moving children toward pre-defined outcomes, we risk creating a productivity-based approach to childhood, one where every experience is expected to serve learning. While learning through experience and play is valuable, it is not the only thing children need.

Children need unhurried childhoods with a range of experiences, including rest, movement, and time that is not directed toward any particular goal. Central to this is recognising that children naturally move between different energy states depending on what they need in any given moment. For example, one child after lunch might settle into slow, stretchy movement; another might enter a state of deep, absorbed play, what we might call flow, which is itself a form of rest. Neither is more productive than the other. and both are necessary parts of a child's everyday rest-full experiences.

Put it into practice: Wall coverings in settings

Walls should only have 25 per cent of covering otherwise the 'visual noise' can compete for attention (Wass and Goldenberg, 2025).

The default network – aka the rest network

> As a general rule, the more time you spend doing nothing, the better it is for your brain.
>
> Jebelli, 2025, p. 4

One of the reasons we both became early educators is not because all you get to do is play all day, but because we both loved the freedom that is often associated with early childhood education (a freedom that is increasingly being diminished by terrible educational policies). It is not for everyone because the role is labour-intensive and requires getting comfortable with often not knowing which direction the children will take you in on any one day. One minute you are talking about the multiple variations of penguins, the next you are consoling a child who is experiencing the great injustices of a snatched toy. Working with children requires a capacity for uncertainty, being regularly met with questions you cannot answer, while holding the tension between teaching and respecting the integrity of children's unruly worlds.

Incorporating rest across early education is not a luxury; it is a necessity if we are to create enriching spaces where children can actually learn. I recently read *Why Doing Nothing Can Change Your Life: The Brain at Rest* and, while I generally steer away from books that feel like self-help, this book was translatable to how we should be working in the Early Years. Jebelli (2025) refers to our brain's default network which is a circuit of neurons (brain cells that communicate through electrical and chemical signals) that enables us to daydream, mind wander, think reflectively and imagine. This network is at its most active when we are doing nothing, or rather not focusing on or exerting ourselves in a task. It is our roam-free mode. By doing 'nothing', this default network can enhance our intelligence, creativity, social empathy and longer-term productivity (p. 4).

I was recently involved in an intense exchange on social media after suggesting that when humans play, it can be entirely pointless, and that we do not need to be learning through play all the time. My argument was that when we insist on learning as the justification for play, we narrow it into a measure of productivity. Unsurprisingly, this did not land well in a space where people's work is centred on play and on advocating for it, particularly at a time when play itself feels under threat. To be clear, my point was not 'do not advocate for learning through play'. Rather, it was that play should not have to prove its worth through learning outcomes. Play is an innate human behaviour, and it has functions beyond learning.

The counter argument I received was that even in the examples I gave of not learning through play, learning could still be identified. For instance, I explained that one of my personal play patterns is swimming. I swim every day and for me it is a restful and playful experience. I am learning nothing. I already know how to swim. I do not need to improve or master anything. I swim precisely because it does not require too much effortful focus. 'Nothing' does not mean literal absence. It refers to activities that do not demand over-exertion, problem-solving, or performance. They allow the mind and body to settle, wander and restore rather than strive or produce.

These same principles apply to our children. Teaching them how to rest, in ways that match their preferences is not a break from learning, it is part of the learning. With this in mind, Sarah and I wanted to explore what this looks like in practice and to also account for the fact that rest sits within a wider spectrum of flow states and energetic states and we need to make room for all of them.

Defining rest, flow and energetic states

When we go into early childhood settings, we are not looking for 'calm corners', rather we want to know how rest, flow and energic states are accommodated and provided for, recognising that children and adults will move between these across any one day; we focus on access. We define rest, flow and energetic states below.

- *Rest states and spaces*: rest is when our mind, body, emotions, energy and senses need a pause so we can reset and feel steady, safe and less overwhelmed. Rest helps us lower demands, return to balance and find comfort through soothing, predictable or grounding experiences.
- *Flow states and spaces*: flow is when our mind, body, emotions, energy and senses are in a state of absorbed engagement, where demands and supports

are well matched and we feel immersed, steady and connected. Flow helps us sustain attention, deepen play and thinking and remain with what matters to us through continuity, rhythm and meaningful engagement.

- *Energetic states*: energetic states are when our mind, body, emotions, energy and senses need an activating boost so we can feel alert, engaged and ready to explore. Rise helps us build momentum, curiosity and connection through energising, activating or stimulating experiences.

Childhood should not be viewed as a period where children need to be constantly learning or proving their worth or readiness. Childhood is not a race, but a distinct developmental phase where children should be given time to unfold into who they are at a pace that suits them. Across every day, children will need access to rest, flow and energetic states to experience wellbeing and balance.

Put it into practice: Visuals for quiet time

Use visuals or indicators that allow a child to opt for quiet time. For example, have a low-down display or board where children can point to different rest types. Often when children are tired, they do not want the added fatigue of explaining what they need and visuals can be a good gateway to rest.

The principles of rest, flow and energetic states

Now that we have defined rest, flow and energetic states, lets explore the key principles.

Rest states

- Rest is a right, not a reward.
- Children should be given access to rest through their daily experiences; this should be viewed as a necessary entitlement.
- Children's bodies are places of wisdom meaning children are building up an awareness of when they need rest and how.
- Children's bodies communicate needs long before words do. Attuned adults learn to read cues such as withdrawal, stillness, movement or repetition as meaningful information.
- Rest supports engagement, imagination and learning.
- When demands are lowered, children have space to process experiences, feelings and sensations. Rest creates the conditions for creativity, repair and emotional integration.
- Children need spaces where they are not watched, hurried or corrected.

Flow states

- Adults should protect children's flow states rather than redirect them.
- Flow enables children to stay immersed without being pulled away by adult schedules or interruptions. This continuity supports deeper engagement and regulation.
- Flow reduces unnecessary transitions and interruptions.
- Frequent transitions can fragment children's thinking and nervous systems. Protecting flow means questioning which interruptions are truly necessary.
- Flow allows children to stay with what matters to them.
- When children are absorbed in meaningful activity, they are communicating interest, need and regulation. Flow honours children's priorities rather than replacing them with adult agendas.
- Learning does not need to be fast to be valuable. Flow privileges sustained attention, repetition and depth instead of quick outcomes or constant novelty.

Energetic states

- Energetic states need space. Children move between high and low energy throughout the day. They need space to be loud, physical and fully alive in their bodies, just as they need space to be quiet and still.
- Energic states support children to feel alert, activated and embodied without expectations to perform or produce. Energy is valued for how it feels, not how it looks to others.
- Movement is a form of expression and selfhood.
- Children communicate through movement as much as through words. All forms of mobility should be valued and children should feel safe enough to emote through embodiment.
- Children's energetic states are best supported when their unique rhythm is honoured.
- Not all children need the same pace, intensity or timing. Honouring rhythm means responding to individual energy patterns rather than enforcing conformity.

Activity 5.1 Reflect on your approach

- Do you have resources in your continuous provision that enable children to activate their proprioceptive (body awareness) and vestibular (balance and movement) systems? Heavy work baskets, for example, which help children feel grounded and settled in their bodies.
- Reflect on your 'tidy up' routines. Do you need to tidy everything away or can there be spaces and opportunities for children to engage in prolonged play and exploration, and to return to this over days/weeks or longer as needed?
- Do you think about play beyond the notion of learning through play, recognising that children also need to access play as a way of regulating and resting? This also helps you to respect play that doesn't yet make sense or is repetitive in nature.

Behaviour blueprints (old to new way of thinking)

Old blueprint: Behaviour as something to stop

Children's worth is measured by how productive they are …

Due to an increasing emphasis on school readiness and learning through play, it seems we have become very driven by the idea that for a child to have value, they need to prove that everything they do is productive – whether it is the pressures of meeting milestones, following along with expectations and learning through every action and interaction. Children's lives have become more focused on who they will become and how they are proving that they are on the right track. And then we wonder why behaviour might be worsening; it is children letting us know, loudly and clearly, that they need time to be in the moment.

New blueprint: Behaviour as something to understand and resolve

Rest, flow and relaxation are a child's right.

Early childhood is a space in which children will have many enriching and meaningful experiences – and, of course, they will learn, develop, grow and mature. However, for these things to unfold, children also need time to just be. Whether it is through uninterrupted time to play, a softening of rules and expectations that may expect too much of them or an educator gently pushing back against the idea that children need to be getting school ready. This is where we can draw on the lineage of rest is resistance, for both the children and ourselves.

The ten types of rest

Let's look in detail at the ten types of rest. Across the rest of this book, we have explored the need for movement and energetic experiences as part of regulation. In this chapter, we are going to specifically explore the ten types of rest as an alternative to calm approaches. The ten types of rest is influenced and adapted from the work of Saundra Dalton-Smith and the seven types of rest (2017).

1 Sleep and naps

Sleep and naps provide deep restorative rest for the body and brain. In the Early Years, sleep is not a habit to be trained or controlled, but a biological and relational process shaped by safety, rhythm and trust. Children vary widely in their sleep needs across the day; restfulness may look different from child to child.

Remember that sleep in early childhood is supported through predictability, attunement and comfort rather than strict schedules or behavioural techniques. Through gentle routines and environmental care, you might try:

- creating consistent, predictable nap rhythms that reflect children's individual sleep needs;
- offering a calm, low-stimulus sleep space with dim lighting and reduced noise;

- supporting children to wind down through familiar cues such as songs, stories or quiet presence;
- respecting children who need shorter naps, longer naps or quiet rest instead of sleep;
- staying emotionally available during transitions into and out of sleep;
- avoiding rushed wake-ups so children can reorientate gently.

2 Sensory rest

A gentle pause from sensory input. Sensory rest enables the nervous system to settle by reducing input, stimulus and features that may be fatiguing or stressful. Lights, noise, clutter and language can feel high-demand. Sensory rest supports children in restoring comfort and safety within their bodies.

Remember that the sensory environment can compete for the child's attention and resources, leading to fatigue and being disgruntled. Through environmental scanning, you might try:

- turning the 'big lights' off;
- increasing access to natural lighting and green scenes, such as plants or nature;
- reducing background noise or providing 'softening' to absorb sounds – for example, rugs and cushions;
- reducing clutter or visual noise which can be aggravating;
- reducing and limiting language which can just sound like noise;
- giving a child access to their sensory highs (Conn, 2015), glimmers and glows which refers to the feeling evoked by pleasant sensory experiences (Jelenjev, 2024);
- listening to low-demand tunes or chill-out music;
- providing sensory dulling such as noise-cancelling headphones or resting eyes with eye masks.

3 Mental rest

Children will be hearing and engaging with multiple demands a day which can lead to cognitive overload. A break from cognitive and language demands can take the pressure off. Mental rest quiets the thinking brain, reducing questions, instructions and problem-solving tasks. It gives space for children to simply be, without expectation of output or focus.

Reducing mental demands can provide the child with the much-needed head-space to gather their thoughts. Mental rest enables a child to have processing time to re-engage:

- limit language recognising that the child may be overloaded by too much talk;
- switch from direct questioning to gentle declarative statements which place less pressure. For example, instead of saying "are you ready to put your toys away so we can have snack", you might say: "Snack time is coming … I'm going to get things ready.";

- generally reduce demands and instructions;
- provide uninterrupted access to preferred play patterns;
- use gentle modelling and scaffolding where needed – for example, show a child rather than tell them;
- break instructions down with pause points for processing;
- reduce distractions.

4 Social rest

One of the biggest demands on children is to be pro-social, often being expected to share, take turns and be open to socialisation. But this can exhausting for all humans. Time away from social performance and interaction demands is beneficial. Social rest affirms the right to solitude, silence, or parallel presence with others, enabling children to replenish energy that is often drained through constant social navigation.

Be mindful of viewing a child as anti-social when they show visible signs of social fatigue. Being around other humans can be replenishing, but it can also be depleting:

- have solo spaces where children know they can go if they need time away from adults or peers;
- use visuals or indicators that allow a child to opt for quiet time;
- teach children simple scripts to express boundaries – for example, 'my choice right now is to play alone, but maybe later';
- provide headphones or ear defenders to create low-demand time while signalling to others that the child is focused elsewhere;
- offer a card or signal system for children to show 'I need space';
- teach and model the concept of parallel play as a valid form of connection.

5 Playful rest

While play might be the bread and butter of your Early Years practice, it is also important to recognise that not all play has to be linked to learning. Sometimes pointless play is necessary for children to decompress, check out or process. Having uninterrupted opportunities for solitary, parallel and low-demand play can be soothing to the nervous system.

Offering access to playful rest means recognising that not all play has to be linked to pre-defined learning, and sometimes children just need time to wallow in play as a way of being in the moment without expectation or pressure.

You could try:

- offering rhythmic playful opportunities where children can engage in repetitions and patterns that feel soothing for their minds and bodies;
- having gentle music playing in the background so that children know playful rest is available to them;

- developing a list of children's interests and noticing what they are drawn to at different points in the day. These choices can reveal their natural rest pauses. For example, a child who lies down during small world play may be signalling a need for playful rest.

6 Active rest

Movement can be an integral aspect of rest – for example, rest through rhythmic movement. Active rest replenishes and distributes energy by engaging the body through stretching, dancing, heavy work, or outdoor play. Active rest gives much-needed soothing to our vestibular (balance), proprioceptive (body awareness) and interoceptive (internal signals) systems.

Restricting movement when it is needed can lead to escalating stress and dysregulation. The body often has to 'knead' out stress through engaging in movements that feel soothing:

- have spaces to stretch, push, pull, squeeze and elongate;
- offer open-ended spaces to move creatively and actively;
- offer 'heavy work' opportunities – for example, access to a heavy work basket (lifting, pushing and carrying activities that support body awareness and grounding);
- encourage or offer dancing to favourite tunes;
- provide different-paced music for different-paced movements;
- offer rhythmic and repetitive play that involves movement, such as building blocks or kneading playdough.

7 Creative rest

Creative rest is the state of giving your mind, senses and imagination space to breathe, wander and replenish without pressure to produce anything. Creative rest is less about what children make and more about the freedom to get lost in the making.

Creative rest grows when children have space to daydream, imagine and follow their own curiosity without any pressure to produce. You could support creative rest by:

- having creative materials within the continuous provision, such as a range of art or creative books;
- utilising art therapy techniques to support children to engage creatively as a way of processing, regulating or decompressing;
- identifying children's creative interests and ensuring they are made available throughout the day;
- providing creative prompts for children – for example, making up stories or using story dice to get creative juices flowing;
- embracing all forms of creativity and introducing novel ways of creating – for example, pottery or knitting.

8 Emotional rest

Feeling and making sense of emotions and sensations in early childhood is a rollercoaster. Firsts, highs, lows and plateaus are all happening and feeling all the feels can be tiring. Children are also expected to show their emotional growth, but sometimes, time needs to be given to rest, repair, recover and engage with the repertoire of regulation rhythms.

Children need to develop comfort in sitting with emotions and feelings in order to learn how it feels for them uniquely, but also how to resolve and regulate. However, *rest-fullness* is important in pacing the spacing those emotions:

- hugging a soft toy or cuddling up with a blanket;
- sitting quietly with someone you trust;
- listening to a soothing song or gentle music;
- having a 'quiet moment' in a safe, cosy spot;
- reading a story that makes you feel safe;
- wrapping yourself like a burrito and taking deep breaths.

9 Spiritual rest

Spiritual rest in early childhood is about slowing down and reconnecting with a sense of meaning, wonder and presence. It supports children to feel grounded, orientated and connected beyond immediate demands or expectations. Spiritual rest may be linked to faith or belief, but it can also be rooted in connection with the present. It often shows up in quiet noticing, awe and stillness.

You might try:

- spending unstructured time outdoors noticing light, weather or movement;
- sitting quietly together without conversation or tasks;
- providing the child with access to their faith-based experiences such as prayer;
- watching natural phenomena such as rain, clouds, shadows or leaves;
- offering gentle sensory experiences such as candlelight, soft fabrics or calming sounds;
- creating spaces for stillness where children can simply be present;
- allowing moments of quiet absorption without interruption or explanation.

10 Embodied rest

Embodied rest is the space where children can reconnect with their bodies, sensations and internal rhythms in a way that feels grounding and safe. Early childhood is full of sensory highs, lows and constant movement, and children often experience these sensations with great intensity. Embodied rest gives children time to slow down, notice what their body feels like and find comfort.

It is useful to bring children's awareness to their internal sensations and bodily experiences which helps them to develop a deeper grasp of being within the body. You could try:

- providing warm and cool items (warm cloth, cool stone, warm water bowl) and letting children explore what each sensation feels like inside their body;
- having water and snack stations that children can access independently, supporting them to notice sensations of hunger, thirst or fullness;
- using simple visuals or symbols for 'full of energy', 'slow energy', 'tired energy' and inviting children to choose how their body feels in the moment;
- a soft toy placed on the chest or tummy helps children notice their breathing rising and falling without instruction or correction;
- modelling language like 'My tummy feels fluttery when I'm excited' or 'My shoulders feel tight when I'm worried' to help link internal cues to emotional meaning.

Activity 5.2 Thinking through types of rest

On a piece of paper, list the ten types of rest explored above. For each type, reflect on the following questions. Notes down your thoughts.

- Where does this show up for children?
- Where does this show up for adults?
- Is it planned, permitted or missing?
- Who does this work well for? Who might it exclude?

Now, explore and reflect in more depth. Consider the following:

- Which types of rest are strongly embedded?
- Which types only happen after distress?
- Which types are absent?
- Where is rest expected to be self-managed rather than supported?
- How different is the rest landscape for children compared to adults?

Intersectionality insight: Fluctuating capacity

A common curiosity for early educators, parents and carers is how a child can appear to manage something one day, but not the next. For example, yesterday, a child may have seemed able to follow instructions, yet today they appear distressed by the very same demands. This fluctuation can occur across days, hours or even

(Continued)

minutes. While it is often more noticeable in neurodivergent and disabled children, all humans experience fluctuations to some degree.

This is increasingly described as *fluctuating capacity*, a concept that recognises that children do not always have access to their full range of skills and ways of engaging. Capacity can be depleted by a range of factors, meaning that what felt possible at one moment may feel overwhelming at another. A child who followed instructions with ease one day may struggle the next because the sensory environment feels louder, busier or more intrusive, making the same expectations far more demanding and lowering their available capacity.

Capacity can relate to many different areas. *Cognitive capacity* refers to our ability to think, process information, make sense of situations and use executive functioning skills. *Emotional capacity* may fluctuate, affecting a child's ability to access regulation strategies, tolerate frustration or process feelings. *Physical and energy capacity* can also vary, where a child may appear sluggish or depleted at one point, and energetic and engaged at another.

These capacities rise and fall in response to a complex overlap of internal, relational, environmental, sensory, energy and external factors. Children are not always able to tell us which factors are influencing them, and the experience of *capacity loss* can feel as frustrating for the child as it does for the adult observing it. From my own lived experience as an autistic and ADHD adult, there have been days when I could write this book with ease, entering flow state and feeling totally on track. I would come back the next day with the same gusto, would sit down and could barely type out a sentence. Now, while this might happen for everyone, it is the unpredictability of capacity that can become the barrier.

While fluctuating capacity is part of being human, it tends to be more pronounced for neurodivergent and disabled children and for those experiencing ongoing stressors. This is why it is so important that the spaces we create include conditions that support children across varying capacities, rather than expecting children to perform at the same level regardless of how they are feeling or what they are carrying.

Conclusion

The first time we introduced the concepts of rest, energy and flow in the context of supporting behaviour and regulation, educator's shared how much these ideas resonated beyond the idea of simply being calm. This resonated not only in the context of children, but also how important it is for us as educators to find ways to honour our energy states, need for rest and opportunities to be in the flow and moment. This chapter offers an opportunity for you to go back to your setting and to think about how you might accommodate these experiences as a way of giving children access to a range of regulation opportunities that does not require them to be constantly productive. And, most importantly … for you to find time for your own needs and regulation opportunities.

References

Burman, E. (2017) *Deconstructing Developmental Psychology* (3rd ed.). Routledge. ISBN: 9781138846968

Csikszentmihalyi, M. (1990) *Flow: The Psychology of Optimal Experience.* Harper & Row.

Conn, C. (2015) 'Sensory highs', 'vivid rememberings' and 'interactive stimming': children's play cultures and experiences of friendship in autistic autobiographies. *Disability & Society*, 30(8), pp.1192-1206.

Dalton-Smith, S. (2017). *Sacred rest: Recover your life, renew your energy, restore your sanity.* Hachette Book Group.

Dalton-Smith, S. (2019) *The Real Reason Why We are Tired and What to Do About It.* March. www.ted.com/talks/saundra_dalton_smith_the_real_reason_why_we_are_tired_and_what_to_do_about_it

Hersey, T. (2022) *Rest is Resistance: A Manifesto.* Little, Brown Spark.

Jebelli, J. (2025) *Why Doing Nothing Can Change Your Life: The Brain at Rest.* Penguin.

Jelenjev, L. (2024) Glimmers and glows: Little moments, big shifts. Neurodiversity Education Academy, 21 April. Updated 12 May. Available at: https://www.neurodiversityeducationacademy.org/post/glimmers-and-glows-little-moments-big-shifts

Wass, S. and Goldenberg, G. (2025) *Take Action on Distraction: The Definitive Guide to Improving Attention and Focus in the Early Years and Key Stage One.* Bloomsbury.

6

Behaviour is not as simple as ABC

Meaningful mapping for behaviour and regulation

... it's best not to judge our children's reactions automatically but rather to be mindful of where experiences are landing, with compassion and without judgment for them – and for ourselves.

Mona Delahooke, 2022, p. 47

Provocation: ABC charts as a blunt tool

Amira is four and attends nursery. Her key person has become increasingly frustrated because during adult-led routines such as circle time she throws toys, stretches into other children's personal space and becomes visibly distressed, disrupting the group. In response, staff begin completing ABC charts to identify the trigger. The records consistently show that the antecedent is the adult-led expectation to sit and attend, the behaviour is throwing and stretching out, and the consequence is adult correction or closer supervision. From this, the key person concludes that the demand to sit still and pay attention is the cause of the behaviour and arranges for an adult to sit beside Amira to minimise and control it. Over several weeks, however, the behaviour does not reduce. Instead, Amira becomes more frustrated and staff feel overwhelmed.

The bluntness of ABC charts

When we were both EYFS and inclusion consultants, we often advised settings to use ABC (antecedent, behaviour, consequence) charts. At the time, this felt like sensible advice. If educators could notice what happened before a behaviour and how it was responded to, then patterns might emerge and some behaviours could be reduced or eliminated. These types of tools can present as a 'quick fix' for behaviour and make the person feel like they are actively investigating behaviours, but, again, they usually focus too much on observable behaviours rather than underlying experiences.

It was only when we began delivering behaviour training that the bluntness of ABC charts was realised. Educators told us they had accumulated folders of behaviour charts that told them very little about the child. What they did notice, however, was that perceptions of those children were worsening over time. Many educators also shared that low-intensity behaviours were often easy to interpret without the need for formal recording. It meant that those children who had a much deeper need were being subjected to a surface-level tool. It prompted us to question whether our advice to use ABC charts suggested a gap in our own knowledge, allowing it to become a convenient cover for the reality – that we did not know these children. Using an ABC chart in these moments is a bit like using a screwdriver with the wrong head. At first, it looks right. You might be using a crosshead screwdriver when what you need is an allen key. It might work temporarily or budge the screw slightly, but not enough.

In the same way, ABC charts can create the appearance of action. They help adults feel purposeful and organised. Yet they often fail to help us understand what is actually holding a child's behaviour in place. With repeated use, the focus can shift from understanding the child to documenting the behaviour, and the child becomes increasingly defined by what is written about them.

Another issue is ABC charts focus on behaviour in isolated moments, but they rarely account for the wider conditions shaping a child's responses. Ongoing stress, sensory load, relational experiences, fatigue, exclusion and unmet needs sit outside the reach of a simple chart yet fundamentally shape behaviour. For Sarah and I, our discussions on the ABC charts have represented an opportunity to explore alternative ways of mapping behaviours with the right tools. While ABC charts can be useful in limited contexts, they are not designed for the depth of understanding required when behaviour feels persistent, complex, or hard to hold.

The ABC chart brings us back to Chapter 1, where we explored how an over-reliance on observable behaviour can undermine relational approaches. Throughout this chapter, we return to that concern by examining the limitations of ABC charts, while also offering an alternative framework for deepening understanding. Using the BEES framework, we shift the focus from recording behaviour to making sense of it.

Let's return to Amira in the Provocation at the start of the chapter. Although the ABC charts provide a tidy pattern, they do not lead to meaningful change because they isolate behaviour from its wider context. When the team steps back and observes more broadly, a different picture emerges. They notice that Amira approaches circle time energetically rather than avoidantly, and that she usually loves stories in one-to-one contexts. They observe that when she stretches into others' space, she is not seeking to disrupt, but appears to be trying to create space for herself which is consistent with her preference for solitary and proximity play (i.e. observing play from a distance before joining in for short bursts). Staff recognise that in her play she frequently constructs clear physical boundaries, such as lining up bricks to define 'my space' and 'your space'. Within the tightly packed circle, she has no such control. Her throwing appears less like defiance and more overwhelm. The ABC chart had framed the issue as a simple stimulus response rooted in non-compliance with adult demands. What it failed to account for were the ecological factors shaping the moment. For example, Amira is autistic with a distinct sensory profile and preferences, but she is non-speaking, so her communication comes through her actions.

Once staff widen their lens, they adapt the environment rather than attempt to control the behaviour. A key person notes that ABC charts are often about locating the problem in the child, but often there is so much more going on. Children are invited to draw large circles around themselves to mark personal space, flexible seating is introduced and additional space is built into the routine. In doing so, they move beyond a narrow behavioural explanation towards an ecological understanding. The limitation of the ABC chart in this scenario is not that it identified a sequence, but that it reduced a complex, embodied and relational experience to a linear cause and effect model, obscuring what might be happening in the bigger picture. The reality is that there are many low-intensity behaviours where identifying a trigger and response is quite straightforward, but when we pick up an ABC chart, we are usually doing so because there is more going on the ABC chart itself can very rarely handle such complexity. In this chapter, we want to provide you with a way of exploring behaviour non-judgementally and through understanding the bigger picture.

Introduction

Sarah and I have run lots of behaviour training over the years. Educators will often say that they have come along to the training because they want strategies to deal with behaviour. Educators may refer to the behaviours that they find frustrating, or those they they feel stumped by and just need some help. While we give lots of universal strategies, we make one thing clear from the start … *there is no blanket strategy for a behaviour*. Why? Because behaviours serve so many different functions and are quite personal to the child and their lived experience.

The key to supporting behaviour is relational knowledge

Ultimately, we believe you have to truly know a child before you can offer any meaningful advice on their behavioural experiences. Because our education system is still deeply rooted in behavioural principles that prioritise compliance over connection, educators are often placed in the difficult position of overriding their own instincts and knowledge of a child in order to be seen as successful.

We have spoken to many key people who have shared that when a child's behaviour continues over time, they sometimes feel it reflects badly on them as educators, or that they must not know what to do. In reality, the difficulty often lies in the systems and expectations around behaviour management, which can push educators towards blanket strategies rooted in rewards and sanctions. For example, many primary schools still use public behaviour charts, even though these rarely support deeper connection, learning, or co-regulation. When the same approaches are repeated without much change, it is understandable that progress can feel limited. While strategies such as time-out may bring short-term compliance, they do not necessarily support children in developing the social and emotional skills that last in the long term. We need more sustainable ways of supporting behaviours while also ensuring we too remain in tact.

The problem of ABC

For decades, many early educators have been encouraged to use ABC charts as a way of 'understanding' children's behaviour. These charts ask adults to track what happened before, during and after an incident of behaviour, with the hope that patterns will emerge. While this may sound useful on paper, in practice ABC charts are often time-consuming, surface-level, subjective and stigmatising. Human beings rarely flourish when placed under surveillance, or when their difficulties are invalidated and framed merely as problems to be eliminated.

ABC charts are not neutral tools. They come directly from behaviourism – specifically B.F. Skinner's model (1953) of operant conditioning, known as the *three-term contingency* (antecedent → behaviour → consequence). First described by Sidney Bijou in 1968 and later embedded in *applied behaviour analysis* (ABA), ABC charts were designed to identify triggers and reinforcements so that behaviours could be shaped or eliminated (Bijou, 1968). This makes them firmly rooted in compliance-driven approaches rather than child-centred understanding, So what are the issues with ABC charts, and other compliance based practices?

They pathologise expected behaviours

ABC charts pathologise behaviours in early childhood that are entirely expected, developmentally meaningful and rich with insights into a child's inner world. For example, it is natural for a child to express stress physically while their communication identity is still emerging. Children need time to understand that stress is a natural part of growing. If instead of supporting them to respond and communicate, we treat their stress as a problem; they may learn to see their needs as faults rather than important cues.

They overlook diverse development pathways

ABC charts overlook diverse pathways of development and reduce behaviour to a simplistic, one-size-fits-all explanation. This suggests that behaviours are straightforward and universal. While there may be common behavioural experiences, such as biting, the reasons behind them are shaped by a wide range of factors.

They reinforce behaviourism

ABC charts reinforce behaviourism, which takes an at the surface-level, compliance-driven approach to children's behaviour. For example, believing that simply identifying a trigger allows us to control, eliminate, or extinguish a behaviour fails to recognise the complexity of children's experiences and the holistic nature of their development. For example, I was once supporting a child who was hitting out – not because they wanted to hurt others, but because they required more space and movement in their play. It was tempting to use a behaviourist response such as time-out, but I realised that this approach would make him feel even more contained. In that moment I focused on adapting the environment to help resolve the frustration and the hitting reduced significantly. I then was able to engage in some longer-term teaching on personal space and how a child might express their proximity preferences.

They fail to include the child's voice

ABC charts fail to include the child's voice or their right to autonomy. When we take an 'outside looking in' approach to behaviour, we remove vital opportunities to co-regulate and connect. If our focus is solely on controlling, stopping, or eliminating behaviour, the child is left with fewer opportunities to practise self-regulation. For example, when a child is told they must say 'sorry' after upsetting someone, they may quickly comply with the word, but no space is given to explore what 'sorry' feels like or how to repair a relationship. Instead of learning about empathy and repair, the child learns that a single word can get them out of trouble. In that moment I would draw attention to the fact that a child has been upset by an action, and I might model a response recognising that moral development is practiced over time.

They are based on adult interpretations of behaviour

ABC charts are based on adult interpretations of behaviour, without acknowledging that we carry our own biases into those observations. For example, an educator may choose to track a child's behaviour not because it poses any real harm, but because it feels personally frustrating or does not align with normative expectations. For example, a child may hum or make vocalisations during circle time and this may be perceived as disrupting rather than a sign of engagement. In this case, the adult's offence, discomfort or rigid setting expectations rather than the child's developmental needs or communication are prioritised. For example, we each have our own flashpoints – behaviour that personally aggravates us – and we may judge that behaviour more harshly and biased than others.

They assume behaviours are caused by a single factor

ABC charts assume behaviours are caused by a single, immediate factor (the antecedent), when in reality children's responses are shaped by a complex interplay of emotions, regulation, sensory states and environmental influences. For example, if a child has a 'tantrum', ABC charts direct us to look only at what happened just before, such as a transition or the lights being switched on. We may then mistakenly label that moment as the trigger, when in fact the dysregulation could have been activated by something that happened hours or even days earlier, or by multiple factors interacting at once.

They fail to recognise children's strengths

ABC charts fail to recognise children's strengths, healthy habits and the repertoire of regulation strategies they already have. What children need is to be empowered through co-regulation so they can discover responses that are compatible with their needs. ABC charts, however, focus on highlighting where a child is 'failing' rather than building on the capacities they have already established. For example, a child who hums or rocks to stay soothed may have these behaviours recorded as 'disruptive', rather than being recognised as effective self-regulation strategies that could be supported and expanded.

They trick educators into thinking a 'quick fix' is possible

ABC charts trick educators into thinking that behaviour can be quickly turned around. The reality is that some behaviours naturally resolve because they are developmental and contextual, while others take time and support to shift. We do need non-negotiables for safety, but we also need to acknowledge that behaviours serve a valuable function in the moment. For example, you might find that a child swears when they are angry. You absolutely need to look at stimulating alternative ways for them to express that anger, but it is equally important to recognise that the swearing itself is, for many, self-regulation. It tells you something about their outlet, rather than being dismissed simply as bad behaviour. Swearing feels good when we feel angry; if we just look to stop it, the child is left without a stimulating alternative and behaviours may then escalate. I am in no way suggesting we just ignore or allow swearing, rather that we seek to understand its function while trying to find alternatives.

By rejecting ABC charts, I am not suggesting that we ignore behaviours or allow them to go unchecked. Humans have got to learn how to be decent human beings, but they also need to be treated with dignity when they are learning that decency. Co-regulation is about having the compassion to recognise that managing our human behaviours is hard and we need those around us to help hold the weight of all that comes with our sensations, emotions and feelings. Co-regulation is about connecting with a child through healthy boundaries and supportive approaches that guide them towards resolution and nurture an early sense of accountability – helping children understand the effect of their actions, while also supporting them to find developmentally meaningful ways to respond, repair and to draw on a repertoire of self-regulation techniques. Blame, shame and punishment is avoided; instead it's about guiding children towards diverse empathy, connection and responsibility within the safety of collective and co-regulation. So how might we build compassion and curiosity for children's behaviours? This is where our BEES framework comes in.

The BEES framework

While we will not give generic advice about individual children, we do offer a framework to make sense of behaviour, alongside affirming approaches that might then be personalised.

The BEES framework outlines that the origin of outward behaviours is more complex than a child simply choosing to misbehave or be defiant. Behaviours are not always the result of an immediate trigger and may be accumulative based on ongoing stressors or unmet needs. It is important to understand the broader developmental profile of the child and their unique developmental pathway when deciding how to co-regulate alongside the child. This BEES framework is an exploration tool that enables you to think more deeply about behaviour and to identify developmentally meaningful responses. You can also access this full framework at www.diversepathways.org which includes tools and resources.

Behaviours: What behaviours am I seeing?

These are the 'at the surface' actions we notice in children.

Our role is to observe them with curiosity and without judgement, seeing them as information and cues rather than just something to fix.

Energy states: what is their energy state? (high, maintained, low)

This is about the child's level of alertness, arousal, or relaxation at a given time.

We ask: is there a match or mismatch between the child's current energy state and the demands of the environment?

Emotions: what might they be feeling?

Emotions are the feelings that sit beneath behaviour and are closely linked with energy states.

We consider: how might the child be feeling, and how are those feelings shaping the way they act or respond?

Senses: What is the sensory situation?

Every child has a unique sensory profile – their own *sensory blueprint*.

We tune into: what sensory inputs help this child feel regulated and engaged, and what might trigger or disrupt them? Now let's explore each in a bit more detail.

Behaviour mapping

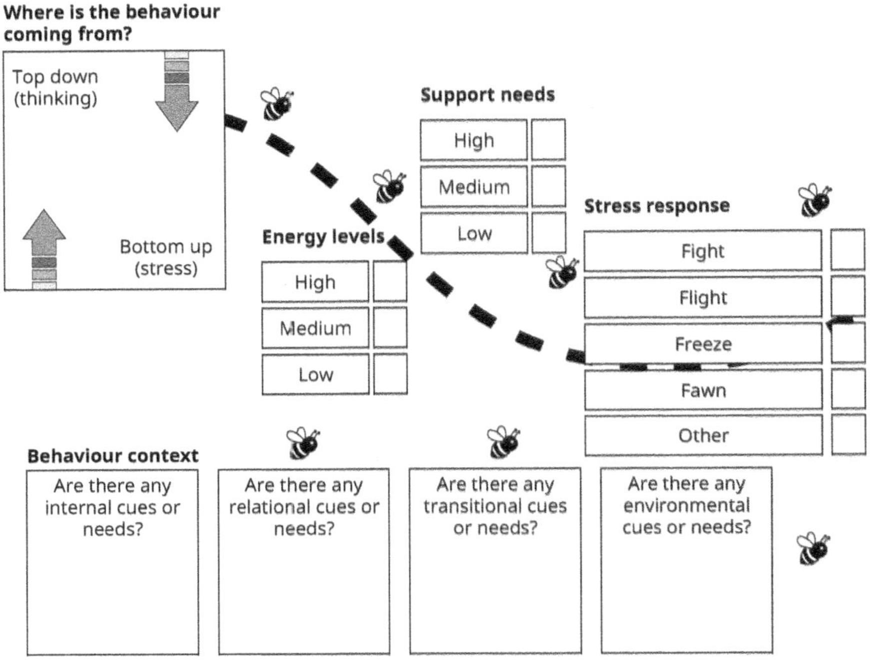

Figure 6.1 An example of a behaviour mapping sheet using BEES

Behaviours

Behaviours are external expressions, and they are happening all the time in early childhood settings. In fact, we should fully accept them as part of learning and development. It is natural to admit that some behaviours feel frustrating or even annoying to us; this doesn't make us bad educators, just human ones.

It is also healthy to talk about behaviours. Sometimes the narrative of going beneath the surface, looking below the tip of the iceberg or going beyond behaviours can feel invalidating when you are in the thick of it trying to support a child who is using every 'at the surface' behaviour to communicate a need, desire, boundary or act of resistance. What we must avoid doing is pathologising or stigmatising children based on natural and expected behavioural occurrences. They form part of our developmental understanding of the child. They also provide us with cues, interactive or non-interactive, about what might be happening and what might be needed. The actions we see may signal stress, frustration, confusion, or unmet needs.

When we observe behaviours, especially ongoing ones, we should do a sense check.

Question one: Is this behaviour bottom-up (stress-driven), top-down (thinking-driven), or a mix of both?

For example, if a two-year-old hits out when another child comes too close during play, I can understand this as the child unconsciously perceiving the other child's presence as a threat. Their body triggers a fight stress response (bottom up), which shows up as hitting. In that moment, the child is not choosing to hurt someone, they are protecting themselves from a perceieved threat. We call this bottom up because it comes from the survival instincts of our brains. Asking them to say 'sorry' at this point is unlikely to be meaningful.

In contrast, I might observe a five-year-old who shouts 'GO AWAY' when peers interrupt his solitary play. Here, he may still feel stress, but he is also consciously recognising that shouting works to protect his play space. This shows more of a top-down response meaning the child can recognise the threat, think about it and decide on an action. In this situation, I would begin planning ways to support him in expressing his need for solitary play in a clearer and more pro-social way. For instance, I might model: 'I can see you like playing on your own. Let's think of another way you can let your friends know without shouting.'

Question two: Is the behaviour the result of an internal, relational, transitional, or external cue?

Behaviour can come from many different places. For example:

- if a child hasn't had a poo that morning (an internal cue), they might feel uncomfortable and out of sorts, as can happen to any of us;
- if their favourite key person is on annual leave and they are with someone they feel less connected to (a relational factor), this might show up in their 'on the surface' behaviours;
- if they are moving from one activity to another and find the change difficult (a transitional factor), their behaviour may reflect the stress of shifting gears or leaving something behind.

Or, if there are lots of children around (an external factor), the environment might simply feel too busy or noisy for them to settle into play.

We won't always get it exactly right, and often behaviour is the result of an accumulation of all these influences. But asking ourselves these kinds of questions can help us narrow down what might be going on for the child.

Question three: Is the behaviour interactive or non-interactive?

One saying I struggle with is 'all behaviour is communication'. Even if there's truth in it, the phrase feels too broad to be genuinely helpful in practice. It can also create pressure on educators to respond to every single behaviour, which isn't always necessary or appropriate.

Instead, I find it more useful to think of behaviour as providing information. From there, I ask: is this behaviour interactive or non-interactive?

Interactive behaviours are when a child is clearly seeking connection – for example, attention-seeking (which is not a negative thing; attention is a basic human need).

Non-interactive behaviours are when the child is signalling that they want space. For instance, just as adults sometimes feel grumpy and don't want repeated questions about whether they're 'okay', children too may simply need time and space rather than engagement.

Energy

Energy is a powerful lens through which to understand behaviour. The founders of Autism Level UP! (Dr Amy Laurent and Dr Jacquelyn Fede) often describe energy as the 'language' of autistic children, highlighting how strongly shifts in energy shape their experiences (Laurent and Fede, 2024). But paying attention to energy states isn't just important for autistic children, it offers valuable insight into how all children (and adults) move through play, learning and regulation.

Energy states in early childhood are the natural fluctuations in a child's alertness, arousal and vitality throughout the day. They shape how children engage, regulate emotions and participate in learning or play. These are not fixed traits, but dynamic shifts in response to internal factors (like sleep, hunger, sensory processing) and external ones (like environment, relationships, or transitions). For example, if a child is low in energy, they may find instructions of external demands more frustrating. Or a child might be high energy and lively, and the idea of sitting still for circle time is not compatible in that moment with their energy state.

Energy states can look like:

- *high energy*: lively, active, excitable, restless, disgruntled, hyperactive;
- *medium energy*: alert, at ease, focused, energised, flow state 'gruntled' (Laurent and Fede, 2024), settled;
- *low energy*: tired, withdrawn, sluggish, disengaged, relaxed.

Recognising these states helps educators adapt expectations, environments and interactions. Supporting children to move flexibly between states is a key part of co-regulation and wellbeing. Trying to suppress energy states will just lead to a child becoming more fizzy inside, and that energy needs to be regulated somehow. Furthermore, energy states relate to us as educators too, and we should be tuning into our own as much as the children's. For example, if I am low energy, I know my capacity to co-regulate might be compromised and so I need to explore what to rest, repair and replenish.

One thing I consider when exploring energy states is what does the child need in that moment:

- *the charging station*: a place to replenish batteries and restore energy. As co-regulators, we often provide children with this vital charge;
- *the spa*: a space for rest, relaxation, quiet and quality time with oneself;
- *the gym*: a space to get active, release energy and move the body;
- when you look around your environment, how are these provided?

(Adapted from Autism Level UP!, presented by Dr Amy Laurent and Dr Jacquelyn Fede at the Yellow Ladybugs Conference, 2025.)

Emotions

Emotions can be complex to navigate at any age. They are not just about naming a feeling, but about the ongoing process of identifying, processing and responding. Simply asking children how they feel, or guessing for them, is not always helpful because, like adults, emotions can be endlessly perplexing. This can be particularly difficult for children who experience *alexithymia*, a difficulty in recognising, distinguishing and describing emotions in oneself. Alexithymia is not uncommon in neurodivergent populations and can make emotional awareness and expression especially challenging without attuned support (Vaiouli, Luminet and Panayiotou, 2022).

Instead, we need to notice the cues their bodies give us. For example, a child who clenches fists, avoids eye contact and paces may not say 'I feel anxious', but their body is offering clear information. Noticing these cues enables us to help draw connections for children. For example, 'Your face is red, and you have tears, could this be anger, or maybe sadness?'

A simple way to think about emotions:

- bodily sensation and interoception (stomach churns, muscles tighten);
- emotion (automatic response system: fight, flight, soothe, seek);
- feeling (conscious awareness plus label: 'I feel nervous').

The process of detecting bodily sensations, developing interoceptive awareness, processing emotions and then consciously attaching meaning to them is challenging at any phase of life. Now imagine being bombarded in that moment with demands such as 'use your words', 'say sorry', 'what's the matter?' or 'calm down'. What children really need is commentary, gentle modelling and patience.

Senses

We are sensory beings, living in a sensory world, each with a unique blueprint for processing and integrating information. When we explore behaviours, energy states, emotions and sensations, it is vital to consider whether we are creating compatible matches or mismatches for children. Ultimately, we must ask: how co-regulating are we, both as people and through the environments we create, especially when it comes to the senses?

It is no exaggeration to say that many of the behavioural observations I have carried out have been alleviated simply by conducting an environmental scan and working towards sensory equilibrium. For example:

- a non-speaking child who frequently screamed outdoors was not angry at all, but distressed by the tickle of her hair in the breeze, a *sensory disruptor*;
- a child who appeared unsettled in a brightly lit room relaxed noticeably once the windows were opened and the lighting was dimmed, giving him space to decompress;
- a child who struggled with visual noise finally settled into story time once the clutter was reduced, allowing him to lie back on a cushion and engage with ease.

There is no magic bag of strategies

A significant turning point for me was realising that I didn't need to be reactive to behaviours or constantly search for strategies to stop them. Over years of using the BEES framework, I came to understand that co-regulation is an active, dynamic and flexible process – one that requires us to zoom out and see beyond the immediate behaviour. For me, this shift has brought greater ease with children's behaviours and reduced the judgement I attach to my own feelings about them. I can now observe a behaviour and acknowledge 'I find this incredibly annoying' without labelling the child – instead recognising that, as humans, we all experience gaps between our emotions and our responses and that our role is to help bridge those gaps.

Behaviour blueprints (old to new way of thinking)

Old blueprint: Behaviour as something to stop

'All behaviour is communication.'

It may seem somewhat controversial to avoid the concept of 'all behaviour is a form of communication', but the reality is that I rarely found it helpful as a statement when I was in the thick of trying to co-regulate. It also feels like an over-generalisation and provides little scaffolding for offering meaningful support. I am not saying it is not a true in many cases, but I think we need other scaffolds.

Humans are complex. While I completely agree that connection and shared understanding matter, I have always found 'all behaviour is communication' a bit overwhelming, as if I need to decode and interpret every single behaviour or uncover the meaning underneath. The truth is, sometimes we just don't know. In those moments, we might consider what information it provides and plan accordingly.

New blueprint: Behaviour as something to understand and resolve

'All behaviour gives us information.'

Behaviour gives us information, but not all behaviour intends to communicate or needs an interactive response.

Interactive behaviours are those where the child is seeking attention, connection, help, guidance, support, scaffolding, or co-regulation.

For example, a child pulling at another child's coat while looking towards their key person might be interpreted as an interactive behaviour – a sign they need connection or support.

Non-interactive behaviours are those where the child needs to decompress, retreat, escape, hide, reject, avoid, or rest from their experience.

For example, a child who screams and runs off when a key person asks 'What's the matter?' or 'Can you use your words?' might be showing a non-interactive behaviour. In that moment, we can rely on the environment to support co-regulation – for instance, by offering a rest space or den.

Put it into practice: From behaviour management to behaviour attunement

So how does a movement from *behaviour management* to *behaviour attunement* look in practice? Below are some examples of externalised behaviours. For each, we outline the behaviour management approach; we then aim to 'make sense' of the behaviour using a BEES approach. In the final column, we suggest how behaviour attunement may look in this scenario.

Table 6.1 Moving from behaviour management to behaviour attunement

Externalised behaviour	Behaviour management	Sense-making	Behaviour attunement
Two-year-old child hits out at a child playing nearby	Tells the child off and explains that it is not nice to hit. Places on time-out	The child notices another child nearby and perceives this as a potential threat to their play. This could indicate that the child's amygdala has been triggered. The child enters a fight reaction and impulsively hits out at the other child	By age two, the child may have shown a stress response, acting to protect their play space. The educator can acknowledge this reaction and help re-establish a safe, uninterrupted play environment for the child

(Continued)

Table 6.1 (Continued)

Externalised behaviour	Behaviour management	Sense-making	Behaviour attunement
The child has several wet accidents a day because they appear to forget to go to the toilet	The child is told off for not going to the toilet and told they are old enough to know better	Children are developing interoceptive awareness in their Early Years and can sometimes become so immersed in play that they do not register their bodily sensations	Provide regular reminders to children during play and demonstrate how certain sensations might feel. Use a visual aid, such as a toilet symbol, to avoid disrupting the child's flow state
The child appears very lazy during routines and avoids any demands	The child is told that they are being defiant and should do as they are told	The child may be experiencing stress or overwhelm, especially if they are avoiding demands	Break tasks into smaller, manageable steps and include opportunities for rest and retreat. Adjust expectations to ensure the child doesn't feel overwhelmed

Intersectionality insight: We are not behaviour detectives

> When we say abolish police, we also meant the cop in your head and in your heart.
>
> Tourmaline, 2020, cited in Beneke and Love, 2025, p. 129

We have been writing this book at a time when geopolitics weighs ever more heavily on both of us. There is often an expectation on educators to not be political, and to remain neutral. We reject this notion as we believe that it legitimises harm, allowing it to go unchecked, in exchange for comfort and palatability. As two white educators, we have actively worked to ensure we use our privilege wherever and however possible. This book is no exception. We are writing this book during a period of profound instability for children's rights. Across the world, children are being directly affected by political and global events. Where there is advocacy and resistance, there is also policing and surveillance. You might be thinking 'What does this have to do with behaviour, or my setting?' We cannot write about behaviour, power and childhood without acknowledging this wider context. What we choose to accept, overlook, or normalise does not stay contained within the places that it happens. It filters into institutions, policies and everyday practices, including early childhood education spaces. We must remain attentive to what becomes usualised in our communities when behaviours, systems and language go uninterrogated.

Sarah and I have discussed this at length in relation to policing metaphors in education, including the suggestion that we are 'behaviour detectives'. While often used as metaphor for investigating behaviour, this language draws on policing metaphors that openly position adults as investigators and children as suspects. When combined with tools such as ABC charts, or behaviourist techniques such as time-out, the focus can shift towards surveillance, evidence gathering and behaviour tracking, rather than relationship, context and care.

This matters because language is not neutral. Policing metaphors sit within wider systems that already disproportionately impact certain groups of children. We know that Black children are more likely to experience adultification and harsher interpretations of their behaviour. Furthermore, neurodivergent children are more likely to have their behaviour pathologised or misunderstood. When behaviour frameworks prioritise monitoring over meaning, these inequities are amplified rather than challenged.

In this book, we have tried to move away from language and tools that mirror systems of control and compliance. Especially as white educators, we have sat with the discomfort of what the research and lived experiences tell us about the harms of whiteness. We are not detectives gathering evidence, and children are not problems to be solved. Our role is to notice, to wonder and to interpret behaviour with care, compassion and an awareness of how bias and power operate within early childhood spaces.

Conclusion

Within our behaviour blocks model, we have introduced an approach you can draw upon when you encounter behaviour that feels confusing, disorientating or even bewildering. In those moments, we can benefit from pointers that help us to navigate observable behaviours and to explore what might be happening for the child. In our view, behaviours do not need to be overlooked, sidelined or 'looked beyond'. We can see the behaviour and still see the child. From there, we can begin to contextualise what is happening by working through the acronym BEES.

Through BEES, we recognise that children use behaviour as a function for expressing, communicating, resisting or advocating. We then consider the possible emotions at play, alongside the child's energy states and sensory experiences. We also situate BEES within the understanding that behaviour is influenced by internal, environmental, relational and transitional factors.

By applying this framework, we increase our chances of understanding what might be happening for a child beyond more traditional approaches such as ABC charts, which can too often reduce behaviour to a single moment or focus solely on stopping the behaviour. In this chapter, we have focused on applying the behaviour blocks model with an emphasis on within-child factors.

References

Bijou, S.W. (1968) *Behavior Analysis of Child Development.* Prentice-Hall.

Beneke, M. and Love, H.R. (2025) *Beyond Compliance in Early Childhood Education: Centering Disability, Freedom, and Belonging. Early Childhood Education Series.* Teachers College Press.

Delahooke, M. (2022) *Brain-body Parenting: How to Stop Managing Behaviour and Start Raising Joyful, Resilient Kids.* Hachette.

Laurent, A.C. and Fede, J.H. (2024) *Energy: The Framework, Tools, Strategies, and Logic to Support Regulation.* Autism Level UP!

Save the Children UK (2025) *Gaza: 20,000 Children Killed in 23 Months of War: More Than One Child Killed Every Hour.* 6 September. www.savethechildren.org.uk/news/media-centre/press-releases/2025/gaza-20000-children-killed-23-months-war-more-one-child

Skinner, B.F. (1953) *Science and Human Behavior.* Macmillan.

Vaiouli, P., Luminet, O. and Panayiotou, G. (2022) Alexithymic and autistic traits in children and adolescents: A systematic review of the current state of knowledge. *Autism.* Feb, 26(2): 308-316. doi: 10.1177/13623613211058512. PMID: 35109700.

Conclusion

The building block of belonging

> Belonging refers to a psychological feeling, and not a mere formal assignment to a social group
>
> Schaffer, 2006, p. 80

When we had our concluding conversations about this book on behaviour, we both knew we had avoided a certain topic throughout. 'Belonging' is a term we hear a lot in education now, but we realised we feel quite complicated about it. This book has been written as a general guide to children's behaviour, but both of our specialisms are caring for and educating children who are neurodivergent and disabled – and, as you have seen through the intersectionality insights, who gets to belong is often conditional. Ultimately, we both believe that our current education systems are not built for belonging, they are built for conformity. While we long for belonging, its sits uncomfortably for us when we see so many children excluded, othered, marginalised or shamed for their complex and diverse human behaviours. Yet we both know it is of crucial importance. So, we decided to end this book on a few meanderings on belonging.

Gere and MacDonald (2010) argue that the *need* to *belong* has one of the strongest effects on our emotions, thinking and behaviours. If this need goes chronically unmet, it can have many negative consequences, and this can profoundly affect our lives. But a key question we have to ask ourselves is whether or not we create spaces where children can actually belong? When we think of behaviour and the intolerance for it in our schooling system, we keep coming back to the same thinking: belonging is conditional and its existence is usually defined by adults, rather than the children themselves. Several researchers have noted that it is a complex term intertwined with issues of othering, exclusion and conformity. For instance, according to Souto-Manning et al. (2021), belonging often hinges on children adhering to a set of normative standards. Essentially, one belongs if one 'fits in' with the surrounding group. Yet, we know that the groups of children we care for and educate are vastly diverse in their identity, ways of being and development. However, the pathway to belonging might be less about the child meeting your behavioural expectations, and more the need for us to expand our understanding of why those behaviours are occurring in the first place. In short, belonging doesn't occur because misbehaviours have stopped. Belonging occurs because children can use their behaviours as a way of signalling their needs, wants, resistance, desires and motivations without fear of punishment, othering or exclusion. Through welcoming that signalling, we find ways to connect with children on a deeper level that takes us beyond conformity into attunement.

Do we accept children for all of who they are?

When we shift our focus away from solely trying to stop certain behaviours, we create opportunities to genuinely understand and connect with children as individuals. Often, we perceive Early Years settings as places where children 'become' who they are, inadvertently disregarding the fact that they already have a full identity. According to Shevrin Venet, our responsibility lies in recognising and valuing children in their entirety as individuals who hold significance. This involves refraining from labelling and excluding those who may not conform to our preconceived notions of how education should be conducted (Venet, 2023, p. 90). Embracing this perspective requires accepting children in their complete humanity, including aspects that we may not fully comprehend or that challenge our capacity for co-regulation.

What are the consequences for those children who do not feel a sense of belonging?

According to Caroline Bath (2009) 'forms of discrimination exist to police the borders of belonging' (p. 19). These borders paint a much darker picture about how we live together in the classroom, in our communities and the world at large. I often draw on examples of intervention, and how we can frequently rely on strategies that aim to eliminate the behaviour of a child for the convenience of others. For example, sitting alongside a child during circle time to keep her still is about the child not disrupting the rest of the group rather than being focused on the individual child's need to move. It is within these moments that the child's sense of belonging is predicated on fitting in. So, while they may have enforced belonging to the group, the question remains as to whether they have the pyschological feeling of belonging. The consequences for children who do not belong are far reaching, and may result in additional needs-based or distressed behaviours. For example, neurodivergent children may realise who they are is not welcome and they may mask, conceal or hibernate aspects of themselves.

We want to end with a quote shared with us by David Cahn of Free to Learn Childminding, which he often returns to when thinking about belonging. Alongside this, we draw on Sumsion and Wong's (2011) metaphor of Russian dolls to describe belonging as something that is built through a *nestled-in* approach, where layers of safety, care and connection are held within one another.

David frequently references the work of Early Years educator Bev Bos, whose definition of belonging remains deeply influential. A child's race, class, disability, gender, neurotype and lived experience shape how this belonging is experienced and sustained. As Bos describes:

> Belonging for young children is being in a place where they feel comfortable enough to play without having to look over their shoulders seeking approval or dodging disapproval, to explore without fear, to redefine their space, and to use materials found around them to create for themselves a sense of order, pattern, and structure.
>
> Attributed to Bos, n.d.

Read alongside Sumsion and Wong's (2011) nested model, this definition reminds us that belonging is not a single act or feeling, but something that is layered, relational and continually held in place through the conditions we create around children.

- *Emotionally*: Do we accept the spectrum of emotions that children bring into the setting as part of their learning about those emotions?
- *Socially*: Do we consider the benefits, challenges and barriers of social diversity and being a part of group. Do we cultivate an understanding of difference?
- *Culturally*: Do we attempt to learn about the different bodies of knowledge that children bring to the setting? Do we position a child as a 'knower' in their own worlds.
- *Spatially*: Do we consider the space child occupy? Are we aware of the power balances that can exist within a space (mine, yours, ours) and how these impact on belonging?
- *Temporally*: Are the routines and rhythms in tune with the child? Do we consider flexible timings so that we can account for fluctuating needs?
- *Physically*: Are the environmental features, furniture, resources and artefacts compatible with the child's needs? Does the physical environment cultivate interdependence and autonomy?
- *Sensorially*: Does the child communicate a sense of mind and body synchronicity?
- *Ethically*: How does the space cultivate consent, choice and dignity?
- *Politically*: Is the wider social, political, intersectional and economic climate considered in how belonged the child feels within the setting and community?
- *Legally*: Are the child's rights and needs upheld and in line with their entitlements?

Not only does the child have to belong, but also the behaviours they bring with them. And that is the way to hold belonging as something unconditional.

References

Bath, C. (2009) *Learning to Belong: Exploring Young Children's Participation at the Start of School*. Routledge.

Bos, B. (n.d.) Belonging for young children is being in a place where they feel comfortable enough to play without having to look over their shoulders seeking approval or dodging disapproval, to explore without fear, to redefine their space, and to use materials found around them to create for themselves a sense of order, pattern, and structure. Attributed quotation.

Gere, J. and MacDonald, G. (2010) An update of the empirical case for the need to belong. *Journal of Individual Psychology*, 66(1), 93–115.

Schaffer, H.R. (2006) *Key Concepts in Developmental Psychology*. Sage.

Souto-Manning, M., Ghim, H. and Madu, N.K. (2021) Toward early literacy as a site of belonging. *The Reading Teacher*, 74(5), 483–92.

Sumsion, J. and Wong, S. (2011) Interrogating 'belonging' in belonging, being and becoming: the Early Years learning framework for Australia. *Contemporary Issues in Early Childhood*, 12(1), 28–45.

Venet, A.S. (2023) *Equity-centered Trauma-informed Education*. Routledge.

Co-regulation and collective regulation chart

Please refer to the chart below to find out how we defined each of the situations found in Activity 2.1 on page XX.

Example	Co-regulation	Collective regulation	Why?
An adult sits beside a distressed child, matching their breathing and offering quiet reassurance	✓		The adult has recognised that the child needs support with their emotions and provides a regulation scaffold to the child through a calming and reassuring response
The whole group sings a familiar song to support a transition between activities		✓	The familiar routine and rhythm of the song helps the children to feel safe and reassured as to what is happening next. This shared routine supports collective regulation
A practitioner lowers their voice and slows their movements during tidy-up time, and the room gradually settles	✓	✓	This example could be seen as a blend of both co-regulation and collective regulation. The practitioner is supporting the regulation of the group during a transition time by using calming actions. Similarly, this could be an established shared routine that supports collective regulation
Children copy one another's movements during an energetic outdoor game		✓	In this example, the children are engaged in shared and reciprocal interactions which support them to feel connected, key features of collective regulation
An adult adjusts the lighting and noise level in the room after noticing rising agitation across the group	✓		The adult is attuned to the behaviour and energy state of the group and responds by making adjustments within the environment as part of co-regulation
A child leans into a peer during story time for comfort	✓		Co-regulation often involves peers, as children seek and provide relational support from and for each other

Example	Co-regulation	Collective regulation	Why?
The group follows a predictable routine with some rules that helps everyone know what is coming next		✓	The existence of a familiar routine helps to shape the rhythm and flow of a settings community, and to provide reassurance, safety and connection for everybody in it
An adult supports one child to step away from the group when things feel overwhelming	✓		The adult is providing a clear model for regulation and supporting the child to organise their response to an emotion
Children laugh together during shared messy play, becoming more animated and engaged		✓	Shared joy is an important part of developing feelings of safety and connection. In this example, the children are engaging in shared emotional, sensory and energy rhythms which helps them to collectively regulate
A practitioner offers a hand squeeze or shared rhythm to help a child through a difficult moment	✓		The practitioner is directly facilitating co-regulation through their responsive actions, likely informed by their knowledge of the child and what supports regulation

Index